The Phœnix Nest

1593

Shearsman Classics Series Vol. 8
(Tudor Miscellanies Vol. 2)

The Shearsman Classics series:

1. *Poets of Devon and Cornwall, from Barclay to Coleridge* (ed. Tony Frazer)
2. Robert Herrick *Selected Poems* (ed. Tony Frazer)
3. *Spanish Poetry of the Golden Age in contemporary English translations*
   (ed. Tony Frazer)
4. Mary, Lady Chudleigh *Selected Poems* (ed. Julie Sampson)
5. William Strode *Selected Poems* (ed. Tony Frazer)
6. Sir Thomas Wyatt *Selected Poems* (ed. Michael Smith)
7. *Tottel's Miscellany* (1557)
8. *The Phœnix Nest* (1593)

Forthcoming in the same series:

9. *England's Helicon* (1600)

The Phœnix Nest
1593

edited by
'R.S. of the Inner Temple'

Shearsman Books
Exeter

This edition published in the United Kingdom in 2010
by
Shearsman Books Ltd
58 Velwell Road
Exeter
EX4 4LD

http://www.shearsman.com/

ISBN 978-1-84861-104-7

The Phœnix Nest was first published in 1593, printed by John Jackson,
and compiled by "R.S. of the Inner Temple, Gentleman";
a second edition followed in 1614.

THE PHOENIX NEST.

Built vp with the most rare and refined workes of Noble
men, woorthy Knights, gallant
Gentlemen, Masters of
Arts, and braue
Schollers.

Full of varietie, excellent inuention, and singular
delight.

Neuer before this time published.

Set foorth by R.S. of
the Inner Temple
Gentleman.

Imprinted at London, by
Iohn Iackson.
1 5 9 3

This Booke containeth these 14. most speciall and woorthie workes.

1 The dead mans Right.
2 An excellent Elegie, with two speciall Epitaphes vpon the death of sir Philip Sydney,   pag.1.
3 The praise of Chastitie,   12
4 A Dialogue betweene Constancie and Inconstancie,   16
5 A Garden plot,   21
6 A Dream of Ladies & their Riddles,   23
7 The Chesse play,   28
8 Another rare Dreame,   31
9 An excellent Passion,   63
10 A notable description of the World,   77
11 A Counterloue,   80
12 A description of Loue,   90
13 A description of Iealousie,   91
14 The praise of Virginitie,   93

With other excellent and rare Ditties.

[Original contents page, which featured only those poems with titles. The page numbers do not apply to this edition.]

A Preface to the Reader vpon the dead mans Right.

I Write not (gentle Reader) to flatter, for the dead are not vainglorious: nor to gain, they reward not trauels: for pride lesse, they are other mens vertues not mine owne that I publish: for malice least of all, bicause I see how ill it becomes them to whom I write. But I write to admonish, and (if it might be) to amend vile and enuious toongs: if not, I seekeno other hire nor glorie than the satisfaction of mine owne conscience, by discharging the dutie of a Christian. So fare you well.

The dead mans Right.

*Written vpon the death of the Right Honorable the
Earle of Leicester.*

IT is not vnknowne how wicked Libellors haue most odiouslye sought the slander of our wise, graue, and Honorable superiours: diuulging defamatorie Libels, so full of immodest railings and audacious lies, as no indifferent Reader but may easily discouer their enuie, and iudge of the veritie: The Authors whereof, though in the qualitie of their offence (tending wholie to sedition) they haue woorthily deserued death, yet the substance of their Pamphlets haue not merited answere.

For want whereof some as euill affected as themselues, to whose hands mostly such bookes haue come, are flattered with a poore aduantage, imputing the wise and silent disgesting of such inhonest and scurilous cartels to their guiltinesse: when (simple as they are) who is else so foolish as knoweth not if all diuulged were true, how easily Authoritie might excuse them, hauing pens and Presses at commandement, and power to patronize: Much more when so vntrue as themselues ashamed of their falshoodes, dare not auouch them vnder their owne names being without reach and feare of Authoritie.

Amongst others, whose Honors these intemperate railors haue sought to scandalize, none haue more vildly bin slandered than the late deceased Earle, the godly, loiall, wise, and graue Earle of Leicester: Against whom (void of all iust touch of dishonor) they forged millions of impieties, abusing the people by their diuelish fictions, and wicked wresting of his actions, all to bring his vertues & person in popular hatred.

Which though he during his life meekely bare as a man vntouched, without publishing defence of his innocencie. Yet because the toongs of men irritated to enuie by the instruments of those libellors, being without feare of controlment, sith his death are become ouer scandalous and at too much libertie. It shall not be amisse to perswade more modestie and pietie of speech.

And for as much as I perceiue the greatest and most generall obiection they haue to blemish his honor, is but an opinion of his ambition and aspiring minde, wherewith the capitall and cardinall Libellor of them all hath cunninglie infected the ignorant that knew not the state of his honors: Let vs see how he may iustly be touched.

Did he euer assume vnto himselfe anie vaine or vnlawfull tytle, or was vnsatiate of rule? Did he purchase his honors otherwise than by his vertues, or were they so extraordinarie, as nowe or in times past they haue not beene equaled in others inferior vnto him in condition of birth, and more in desart? If not? I maruell the father of this pestilent inuention blush not as red as his cap, and his children be not ashamed of his falsehood.

Admit this woorthie Earles and our most gratious Souereigne who wisely iudged of his vertues, and worthily rewarded his loialtie and paines, did honor him with titles aboue others of his time: (in humble and seemely sort, I speake it without comparison) who euery way was more fit for the dignitie he bare, and more complet to accomplish them: whereof the Libellor could not be ignoraunt, but that too much yeelding to his malice, he sought to slaunder this notable testimonie of his Excellencie.

Such rather woulde I iudge ambitious, as for promotions whether Ecclesiasticall or Temporall, hauing once conceiued a hope of greatnesse, without regard of conscience or Countrie, with voluntarie hazarde of all things pursue the same, by shamefull, traiterous, and vngodlie meanes, exasperating their naturall Prince and superiour Magistrates by rebellious and seditious Libels. These be the true tokens of an aspiring minde, whose nature is to hinder by malice, where it can not hurt by power.

But leauing further pursute of their malice, I will remember this Earles woorthinesse. For the first and principall vertue of his vertues, his Religion, it shall be needlesse to speake much, sith all Christendome knows he professed one Faith, and worshipped one onely God, whom he serued in vprightnes of life, and defended with hazard thereof in armes and action against his enimies. How he succoured and relieued distressed members of the Church, I leaue to those that haue made proofe, who ought in dutie to make relation thereof.

Next I thinke there is none that will, dare, or can impeach his loialtie, either in fact or faith, sufficiently testified by hir Maiesties gratious loue to whom that belonged, as also by his dutifull and carefull seruice vnto hir. So as further narration thereof shall not neede.

His wisedome by the grauitie of his place, the causes he managed, and the cariage of his person, is approoued not onely vnto vs, but to most nations of the world.

Lastlie of his valour and affection to his Countries peace, no honest minde but is satisfied: whereof what greater testimonie can we require than the trauels his aged bodie vndertooke, and dangers the same was subiect vnto in the warres of the Low Countries, where he voluntarily offered his person in combate against the deuoted enimies of this state and hir Maiestie. Leauing his Wife, possessions, and home, not regarding his safetie, riches, and ease, in respect of the godly, honourable, and louing care he bare the common quiet.

All which the vngratefull Malecontents of this time, on whome any thing is ill bestowed (much more the trauels of so memorable a Noble) spared not to reproch: Hyring the toongs of runawaies and roges, such as neither feare God nor the diuell, or are woorth a home, to proclaime hatefull and enuious lies against him, in alehouses, faires, markets, and such assemblies.

At whose returne when his dealings were truely discussed, and truth ouercame their slanders, this was the refuge of their whispering malice: His greatnesse and smooth toong (saie they) beares it awaie: as if Honor once lost in act, could be hidden by greatnes, or recouered by grace and eloquence of speech. Both which taken away by his happie death, and our vnhappie losse, he is sithence more cleared than before.

Maruell not then at their enuie, sith, *Virtutis comes inuidia*, but detest the enuious, that thus blaspheme vertues, whom (for mine owne part) as I see measure their rage, so will I iudge of their affection to the state: for vndoubtedly none but the discontented with the time, or such as he hath iustlie punished for their lewdnesse, will thus calumniouslie interpret his proceedings.

If I meant to write a discourse of this Earles life, or an Apologie in his defence, I would proceede more orderly in repetition of his vertues, and more effectually in answere of their poisoned Libels: But as mine intent at first was onelie to admonish loose toongs (such as mine eares haue glowed to heare of) and forewarne the ouer credulous that are easily abused, hauing finished my purpose, if it effects amendment, I shall be glad, if not, their shames be on their owne heads.

Beseeching God this Realme feele not the want of him alreadie dead, and greater iudgements insue for our vnthankfulnesse.

L E I C E S T E R he liu'd, of all the world admir'd,
Not as a man, though he in shape exceld:
But as a God, whose heauenlie wit inspir'd,
Wrought hie effects, yet vertues courses held,
His wisdome honored his Countries name,
His valure was the vangard of the same.

An Elegie, or friends passion, for
his Astrophill.
*Written vpon the death of the right Honorable sir Philip
Sidney knight, Lord gouernor of
Flushing.*

AS then, no winde at all there blew,
    No swelling cloude, accloid the aire,
    The skie, like glasse of watchet hew,
Reflected Phœbus golden haire,
    The garnisht tree, no pendant stird,
    No voice was heard of any bird.

There might you see the burly Beare,
The Lion king, the Elephant,
The maiden Vnicorne was there,
So was Acteons horned plant,
    And what of wilde or tame are found,
    Were coucht in order on the ground.

Alcides speckled poplar tree,
The palme that Monarchs doe obtaine,
With Loue iuice staind the mulberie,
The fruit that dewes the Poets braine,
    And Phillis philbert there away,
    Comparde with mirtle and the bay.

The tree that coffins doth adorne,
With stately height threatning the skie,
And for the bed of Loue forlorne,
The blacke and dolefull Ebonie,
    All in a circle compast were,
    Like to an Amphitheater.

Vpon the branches of those trees,
The airie winged people sat,
Distinguished in od degrees,
One sort in this, another that,
    Here Philomell, that knowes full well,
    What force and wit in loue doth dwell.

The skie bred Egle roiall bird,
Percht there vpon an oke aboue,
The Turtle by him neuer stird,
Example of immortall loue.
    The swan that sings about to dy,
    Leauing Meander stood thereby.

And that which was of woonder most,
The Phœnix left sweete Arabie:
And on a Caedar in this coast,
Built vp hir tombe of spicerie,
    As I coniecture by the same,
    Preparde to take hir dying flame.

In midst and center of this plot,
I saw one groueling on the grasse:
A man or stone, I knew not that,
No stone, of man the figure was,
    And yet I could not count him one,
    More than the image made of stone.

At length I might perceiue him reare
His bodie on his elbow end:
Earthly and pale with gastly cheare,
Vpon his knees he vpward tend,
    Seeming like one in vncouth stound,
    To be ascending out the ground.

A greeuous sigh foorthwith he throwes,
As might haue torne the vitall strings,
Then downe his cheekes the teares so flowes,
As doth the streame of many springs.
    So thunder rends the cloud in twaine,
    And makes a passage for the raine.

Incontinent with trembling sound,
He wofully gan to complaine,
Such were the accents as might wound,
And teare a diamond rocke in twaine,

After his throbs did somwhat stay,
Thus heauily he gan to say.

O sunne (said he) seeing the sunne,
On wretched me why dost thou shine,
My star is falne, my comfort done,
Out is the apple of my eine,
    Shine vpon those possesse delight,
    And let me liue in endlesse night.

O griefe that liest vpon my soule,
As heauie as a mount of lead,
The remnant of my life controll,
Consort me quickly with the dead,
    Halfe of this hart, this sprite and will,
    Di'de in the brest of Astrophill.

And you compassionate of my wo,
Gentle birds, beasts and shadie trees,
I am assurde ye long to kno,
What be the sorrowes me agreeu's,
    Listen ye then to that insu'th,
    And heare a tale of teares and ruthe.

You knew, who knew not Astrophill,
(That I should liue to say I knew,
And haue not in possession still)
Things knowne permit me to renew,
    Of him you know his merit such,
    I cannot say, you heare too much.

Within these woods of Arcadie,
He cheefe delight and pleasure tooke,
And on the mountaine Parthenie,
Vpon the chrystall liquid brooke,
    The Muses met him eu'ry day,
    That taught him sing, to write, and say.

When he descended downe the mount,
His personage seemed most diuine,
A thousand graces one might count,
Vpon his louely cheerefull eine,
  To heare him speake and sweetely smile,
  You were in Paradise the while.

A sweete attractiue kinde of grace,
A full assurance giuen by lookes,
Continuall comfort in a face,
The lineaments of Gospell books,
  I trowe that countenance cannot lie,
  Whose thoughts are legible in the eie.

Was neuer eie, did see that face,
Was neuer eare, did heare that tong,
Was neuer minde, did minde his grace,
That euer thought the trauell long,
  But eies, and eares, and eu'ry thought,
  Were with his sweete perfections caught.

O God, that such a woorthy man,
In whom so rare desarts did raigne,
Desired thus, must leaue vs than,
And we to wish for him in vaine,
  O could the stars that bred that wit,
  In force no longer fixed sit.

Then being fild with learned dew,
The Muses willed him to loue,
That instrument can aptly shew,
How finely our conceits will moue,
  As Bacchus opes dissembled harts,
  So loue sets out our better parts.

Stella, a Nymph within this wood,
Most rare and rich of heauenly blis,
The highest in his fancie stood,
And she could well demerite this,

Tis likely they acquainted soone,
　　　He was a Sun, and she a Moone.

Our Astrophill did Stella loue,
O Stella vaunt of Astrophill,
Albeit thy graces gods may moue,
Where wilt thou finde an Astrophill,
　　　The rose and lillie haue their prime,
　　　And so hath beautie but a time.

Although thy beautie doe exceede,
In common sight of eu'ry eie,
Yet in his Poesies when we reede,
It is apparant more thereby,
　　　He that hath loue and iudgement too,
　　　Sees more than any other doe.

Then Astrophill hath honord thee,
For when thy bodie is extinct,
Thy graces shall eternall be,
And liue by vertue of his inke,
　　　For by his verses he doth giue,
　　　To short liude beautie aye to liue.

Aboue all others this is hee,
Which erst approoued in his song,
That loue and honor might agree,
And that pure loue will doe no wrong,
　　　Sweete saints it is no sinne nor blame,
　　　To loue a man of vertuous name.

Did neuer loue so sweetly breath
In any mortall brest before,
Did neuer muse inspire beneath,
A Poets braine with finer store:
　　　He wrote of loue with high conceit,
　　　And beautie reard aboue hir height.

Then Pallas afterward attyrde,
Our Astrophill with hir deuice,
Whom in his armor heauen admyrde,
As of the nation of the skies,
    He sparkled in his armes afarrs,
    As he were dight with fierie starrs.

The blaze whereof when Mars beheld,
(An enuious eie doth see afar)
Such maiestie (quoth he) is seeld,
Such maiestie my mart may mar,
    Perhaps this may a suter be,
    To set Mars by his deitie.

In this surmize he made with speede,
An iron cane wherein he put,
The thunder that in cloudes do breede,
The flame and bolt togither shut.
    With priuie force burst out againe,
    And so our Astrophill was slaine.

This word (was slaine) straightway did moue,
And natures inward life strings twitch,
The skie immediately aboue,
Was dimd with hideous clouds of pitch,
    The wrastling winds from out the ground,
    Fild all the aire with ratling sound.

The bending trees exprest a grone,
And sigh'd the sorow of his fall,
The forrest beasts made ruthfull mone,
The birds did tune their mourning call,
    And Philomell for Astrophill,
    Vnto hir notes annext a phill.

The turtle doue with tunes of ruthe,
Shewd feeling passion of his death,
Me thought she said I tell thee truthe,
Was neuer he that drew in breath,

      Vnto his loue more trustie found,
      Than he for whom our griefs abound.

The swan that was in presence heere,
Began his funerall dirge to sing,
Good things (quoth he) may scarce appeere,
But passe away with speedie wing.
      This mortall life as death is tride,
      And death giues life, and so he di'de.

The generall sorrow that was made,
Among the creatures of kinde,
Fired the Phœnix where she laide,
Hir ashes flying with the winde,
      So as I might with reason see,
      That such a Phœnix nere should bee.

Haply the cinders driuen about,
May breede an ofspring neere that kinde,
But hardly a peere to that I doubt,
It cannot sinke into my minde,
      That vnder branches ere can bee,
      Of worth and value as the tree.

The Egle markt with pearcing sight,
The mournfull habite of the place,
And parted thence with mounting flight,
To signifie to Ioue the case,
      What sorow nature doth sustaine,
      For Astrophill by enuie slaine.

And while I followed with mine eie,
The flight the Egle vpward tooke,
All things did vanish by and by,
And disappeered from my looke,
      The trees, beasts, birds, and groue was gone,
      So was the friend that made this mone.

This spectacle had firmely wrought,
A deepe compassion in my spright,
My molting hart issude me thought,
In streames foorth at mine eies aright,
    And heere my pen is forst to shrinke,
    My teares discollors so mine inke.

An Epitaph vpon the right Honorable
sir Philip Sidney knight: Lord
gouernor of Flushing.

TO praise thy life, or waile thy woorthie death,
And want thy wit, thy wit high, pure, diuine,
Is far beyond the powre of mortall line,
Nor any one hath worth that draweth breath.

Yet rich in zeale, though poore in learnings lore,
And friendly care obscurde in secret brest,
And loue that enuie in thy life supprest,
Thy deere life done, and death hath doubled more.

And I, that in thy time and liuing state,
Did onely praise thy vertues in my thought,
As one that seeld the rising sunne hath sought,
With words and teares now waile thy timelesse fate.

Drawne was thy race, aright from princely line,
Nor lesse than such, (by gifts that nature gaue,
The common mother that all creatures haue,)
Doth vertue shew, and princely linage shine.

A king gaue thee thy name, a kingly minde,
That God thee gaue, who found it now too deere
For this base world, and hath resumde it neere,
To sit in skies, and sort with powres diuine.

Kent thy birth daies, and Oxford held thy youth,
The heauens made haste, & staide nor yeeres, nor time,

The fruits of age grew ripe in thy first prime,
Thy will, thy words; thy words, the seales of truth.

Great gifts and wisedome rare imploide thee thence,
To treat from kings, with those more great than kings,
Such hope men had to lay the highest things,
On thy wise youth, to be transported hence.

Whence to sharpe wars sweete honor did thee call,
Thy countries loue, religion, and thy friends:
Of woorthy men, the marks, the liues and ends,
And her defence, for whom we labor all.

There didst thou vanquish shame and tedious age,
Griefe, sorow, sicknes, and base fortunes might:
Thy rising day, saw neuer wofull night,
But past with praise, from of this worldly stage.

Backe to the campe, by thee that day was brought,
First thine owne death, and after thy long fame;
Teares to the soldiers, the proud Castilians shame;
Vertue exprest, and honor truly taught.

What hath he lost, that such great grace hath woon,
Yoong yeeres, for endles yeeres, and hope vnsure,
Of fortunes gifts, for wealth that still shall dure,
Oh happie race with so great praises run.

England doth hold thy lims that bred the same,
Flaunders thy valure where it last was tried,
The Campe thy sorow where thy bodie died,
Thy friends, thy want; the world, thy vertues fame.

Nations thy wit, our mindes lay vp thy loue,
Letters thy learning, thy losse, yeeres long to come,
In worthy harts sorow hath made thy tombe,
Thy soule and spright enrich the heauens aboue.

Thy liberall hart imbalmd in gratefull teares.
Yoong sighes, sweete sighes, sage sighes, bewaile thy fall,

Enuie hir sting, and spite hath left hir gall,
Malice hir selfe, a mourning garment weares.

That day their Haniball died, our Scipio fell,
Scipio, Cicero, and Petrarch of our time,
Whose vertues wounded by my woorthles rime,
Let Angels speake, and heauens thy praises tell.

Another of the same.
Excellently written by a most woorthy Gentleman.

Silence augmenteth griefe, writing encreaseth rage,
Stald are my thoughts, which lou'd, & lost, the wonder of our age,
Yet quickned now with fire, though dead with frost ere now,
Enrag'de I write, I know not what: dead, quick, I know not how.

Hard harted mindes relent, and rigors teares abound,
And enuie strangely rues his end, in whom no fault she found,
Knowledge hir light hath lost, valor hath slaine hir knight,
Sidney is dead, dead is my friend, dead is the worlds delight.

Place pensiue wailes his fall, whose presence was hir pride,
Time crieth out, my ebbe is come: his life was my spring tide,
Fame mournes in that she lost, the ground of hir reports,
Ech liuing wight laments his lacke, and all in in sundry sorts.

He was (wo worth that word) to ech well thinking minde,
A spotlesse friend, a matchles man, whose vertue euer shinde,
Declaring in his thoughts, his life, and that he writ,
Highest conceits, longest foresights, and deepest works of wit.

He onely like himselfe, was second vnto none,
Whose deth (though life) we rue, & wrong, & al in vain do mone,
Their losse, not him waile they, that fill the world with cries,
Death slue not him, but he made death his ladder to the skies.

Now sinke of sorow I, who liue, the more the wrong,
Who wishing death, whom deth denies, whose thred is al to long,

Who tied to wretched life, who lookes for no reliefe,
Must spend my euer dying daies, in neuer ending griefe.

Harts ease and onely I, like parables run on,
Whose equall length, keepe equall bredth, & neuer meet in one,
Yet for not wronging him, my thoughts, my sorowes cell,
Shall not run out, though leake they will, for liking him so well.

Farewell to you my hopes, my wonted waking dreames,
Farewell somtimes enioied ioy, eclipsed are thy beames,
Farewell selfe pleasing thoughts, which quietnes brings foorth,
And farewel friendships sacred league, vniting minds of woorth.

And farewel mery hart, the gift of guiltles mindes,
And all sports, which for liues restore, varietie assignes,
Let all that sweete is, voide? in me no mirth may dwell,
Philip, the cause of all this woe, my liues content farewell.

Now rime, the sonne of rage, which art no kin to skill,
And endles griefe, which deads my life, yet knowes not how to kill,
Go seeke that haples tombe, which if ye hap to finde,
Salute the stones, that keepe the lims, that held so good a minde.

The praise of Chastitie.

Wherein is set foorth by way of comparison, how great
is the conquest ouer our affections,
by G. P. Master of
Arts.

THe noble Romans whilom woonted were,
    For triumph of their conquered enimies,
    The wreathes of Laurell, and of Palme to weare,
In honor of their famous victories,

And so in robes of gold, and purple dight,
    Like bodies shrinde, in seates of Iuorie,

Their names renowmde for happines in fight,
    They beare the guerdon of their chiualrie.

The valiant Greekes, for sacke of Priams towne,
    A worke of manhood, matcht with policie,
Haue fild the world with bookes of their renowne,
    As much as erst the Romane emperie.

The Phrygian knights, that in the house of fame,
    Haue shining armes of endles memorie,
By hot and fierce repulse did win the same,
    Though Helens rape, hurt Paris progenie.

Thus strength hath guerdon, by the worlds award,
    So praise we birth, and high nobilitie,
If then the minde, and bodie reape reward,
    For natures dowre, conferred liberally.

Presse then for praise, vnto the highest roome,
    That art the highest of the gifts of heauen,
More beautifull by wisdomes sacred doome,
    Than Sol himselfe, amid the Planets seauen.

Queene of content, and temperate desires,
    Choice nurse of health, thy name hight Chastitie,
A soueraigne powre to quench such climing fires,
    As choake the minde, with smoke of infamie.

Champion at armes, re'ncounter with thy foe,
    An enimie foule, and fearfull to behold,
If then stout captaines haue bene honor'd so,
    Their names in bookes of memorie enrold,

For puissant strength: ye Romane peeres retire,
    And Greeks giue ground, more honor there is woon,
With chaste rebukes to temper thy desire,
    Than glory gaind the world to ouer run.

Than fierce Achilles got, by Hectors spoyle,
    Than erst the mightie prince of Macedon,

King Philips impe, that put his foes to foyle,
    And wisht more worlds to hold him plaie than one.

Beleeue me to contend 'gainst armies royall,
    To tame wilde Panthers but by strength of hand,
To praise the triumph, not so speciall,
    As ticing pleasures charmes for to withstand.

And for me list compare with men of war,
    For honor of the field, I dare maintaine,
This victory exceedeth that as far,
    As Phœbus chariot Vulcans forge doth staine.

Both noble, and triumphant in their kindes,
    And matter woorthie queene Remembrance pen,
But that that tangles both our thoughts and mindes,
    To master that, is more than ouer men,

To make thy triumph. Sith to strength alone,
    Of body it belongs, to bruze or wound,
But raging thoughts, to quell, or few, or none,
    Saue vertues imps, are able champions found.

Or those whom Ioue hath lou'd? or noble of birth,
    So strong Alcydes, Ioues vnconquered son,
Did lift Achelous bodie from the earth,
    To shew what deeds by vertues strength are don.

So him he foild, and put to sudden flight,
    By aime of wit, the foule Stimphalides?
And while we say he mastered men by might,
    Behold in person of this Hercules.

It liketh me to figure Chastitie,
    His labor like that foule vncleane desire,
That vnder guide of tickling fantasie,
    Would mar the minde, through pleasures scorching fire.

And who hath seene a faire alluring face,
    A lustie girle, yclad in queint aray,

Whose daintie hand, makes musicke with hir lace,
    And tempts thy thoughts, and steales thy sense away.

Whose ticing haire, like nets of golden wyre,
    Enchaine thy hart, whose gate and voice diuine,
Enflame thy blood, and kindle thy desire,
    Whose features wrap and dazle humaine eine.

Who hath beheld faire Venus in hir pride,
    Of nakednes all Alablaster white,
In Iuorie bed, strait laid by Mars his side,
    And hath not bin enchanted with the sight,

To wish, to dallie, and to offer game,
    To coy, to court, & caetera to doe:
(Forgiue me Chastnes if in termes of shame,
    To thy renowne, I paint what longs thereto)

Who hath not liu'd, and yet hath seene I say,
    That might offend chaste hearers to endure,
Who hath bene haled on, to touch, and play,
    And yet not stowpt to pleasures wanton lure.

Crowne him with laurell, for his victorie,
    Clad him in purple, and in scarlet die?
Enroll his name in bookes of memorie,
    Ne let the honor of his conquest die.

More roiall in his triumph, than the man,
    Whom tygres drew in coach of burnisht golde,
In whom the Roman Monarchie began,
    Whose works of worth, no wit hath erst controlde.

Elysium be his walke, high heauen his shrine,
    His drinke, sweete Nectar, and Ambrosia,
The foode that makes immortall and diuine,
    Be his to taste, to make him liue for ay:

And that I may in briefe describe his due,
    What lasting honor vertues guerdon is,

So much and more his iust desart pursue,
   Sith his desart awards it to be his.

L ENV OY.

To thee in honor of whose gouernment,
   Entitled is this praise of Chastitie,
My gentle friend, these hastie lines are ment,
   So flowreth vertue like the laurell tree,
   Immortall greene, that euere eie may see,
     And well was Daphne turnd into the bay,
      Whose chastnes triumphes, growes, & liues for ay.

An excellent Dialogue betwene Constancie
and Inconstancie, as it was by speech presented
*to hir Maiestie, in the last Progresse at
sir Henrie Leighes house.*

Con-stan-cie. **M**ost excellent: shall I say Lady, or Goddesse? whom I should enuie to be but a Lady, and can not denie to haue the power of a Goddesse? vouchsafe to accept the humble thankfulnes of vs lately distressed Ladies, the pride of whose wits was iustly punished with the inconstancie of our ; whereby we were caried to delight, as in nothing more than to loue, so in nothing so much as to change louers; which punishment, though it were onely due to our yet did it light most heauily vpon those knights, who following vs with the heate of their affection, had neither grace to get vs, nor power to leaue vs. Now since by that more than mortall power of your more than humane wisedome, the enchanted tables are read, and both they and we released, let vs be punished with more than inconstancie, if we faile either to loue constantly, or to your memorie.

Inconstancie. Not to be thankfull to so great a person, for so great a benefite, might argue as little iudgement, as ill nature: and therefore though it be my place to speake after you, I will striue in thankfulnes to go before you, but yet rather for my libertie, bicause I may be as I list, than for any minde I haue to be more constant than I was.

Const. If you haue no minde to be constant, what is the benefit of your deliuerance?

Inconst. As I tolde you before, my libertie, which I loue better than my selfe; for though I loue inconstancie as my selfe, and had as leeue not be, as not be vnconstant; yet can I not but hate that which I loue; but when I am enforced vnto it: and (by your leaue) as daintie as you make of the matter, I am perswaded that you would euen hate your selfe, if you were but wedded vnto your selfe.

Const. Selfeloue is not the loue that we talke of, but rather the kinde of knitting of two harts in one, of which sort if you had a faithfull louer, what shoulde you loose by being faithfull vnto him?

Inconst. More than you shall get by being so.

Const. I seeke nothing but him to whom I am constant.

Inconst. And euen him shall you loose by being constant.

Const. What reason haue you for that?

Inconst. No other reason than that which is drawn from the common places of loue, which is for the most part, reason beyond reason.

Const. You may rather call it reason without reason; if they conclude that loue and faith, the more they haue, the lesse they shall finde.

Inconst. Will you beleeue your owne experience?

Const. Farre beyond your reason.

Inconst. Haue you not then found amongst your louers, that they would flie you, if you do but follow them, and follow you most, when you do most flie them?

Const. I graunt I haue found it too true in some, but I now speake of a constant louer indeed.

Inconst. You may better speake of him than finde him; but the onely way to haue him, is, to be vnconstant.

Const. How so?

Inconst. I haue heard Philosophers say, that *Inquisito termino cessat motus*, there is no motion (and you know loue is a motion) but it ceaseth (or rather dieth) when it hath gotten his end; and to say the truth, loue hath no edge when it is assured, whose verie foode and life is hope, and the hope of hauing, is dull without the feare of loosing, where there are no ryuals.

Const. But the more constant he findes me, the more carefull he will be to deserue well of me.

Inconst. You deceiue your selfe with that conceite, and giue him no small aduantage to range where he listeth, when you let him know you are at his deuotion, whom you shall be sure to haue at yours, if by an indifferent cariage of your selfe, you breede an emulation betweene him and others.

Const. It were against nature for hir which is but one, to loue more than one, and if it be a fault to beare a double hart, what is it to diuide the hart among many.

Inconst. I aske no other iudge than nature, especially in this matter of loue, than which there is nothing more naturall, and surely for any thing that I can see, nature delighteth in nothing so much, as in varietie; and it were hard, that since she hath appointed varietie of colours for the eie, variety of sounds for the eare, varietie of meates for the mouth, and varietie of other things for euery other sense, she should binde the hart (to which all the rest doe seruice) to the loue of one any more, than she bindeth the eie to one colour, the eare to one sound, or the mouth to one kinde of meate.

Const. Neither doth she deny the hart varietie of choyse, she onely requires constancie when it hath chosen.

Inconst. What if we commit an error in our choise?

Const. It is no fault to choose where we like.

Inconst. But if our liking varie, may we not be better aduised?

Const. When you haue once chosen, you must turne your eies inward, to looke onelie on him whom you haue placed in your hart.

Inconst. Why then I perceiue you haue not yet chosen, for your eies looke outwarde, but as long as your eies stand in your head as they doe, I doubt not but to finde you inconstant.

Const. I do not denie but I looke vpon others beside him that I loue best, but they are all as dead pictures vnto me, for any power they haue to touch my hart.

Inconst. If they were but (as you account them) dead pictures, I do not doubt, but they would make an other Pigmalion of you, rather than you would be bound to the loue of one onely; but what if that one prooue inconstant?

Const. I had rather the fault should be his than mine.

Inconst. It is a small comfort to say the fault is his, when the losse is yours, but how can you auoid the fault, who can helpe it and will not?

Const. I see no way to helpe it, but by breach of faith, which I hold deerer then my life.

Inconst. What is the band of your faith?

Const. My worde.

Inconst. Your word is but winde, and no sooner spoken than gone.

Const. Yet doth it binde, to see what is spoken, done.

Inconst. You can do little, if you cannot master your worde.

Const. I should do lesse, if my word did not master me.

Inconst. It masters you indeed, for it makes you a slaue.

Const. To none but one, whom I choose to serue.

Inconst. It is basenes to serue, tho it be but one.

Const. More base to dissemble with more than one.

Inconst. When you loue all alike, you dissemble with none.

Const. But if I loue many, will any loue me?

Inconst. No doubt there will, and so much the more, by how much the more they are that striue for you.

Const. But the hart that is euery where, is indeede no where

Inconst. If you speake of a mans hart, I grant it to be true; but as for the hart of a woman, it is like a soule in a bodie; *Tota in toto, & tota in qualibet parte:* that though you had as many louers, as you haue fingers and toes, you might be but one amongst them all, and yet wholy euery ones: but bicause I see you are peruersly deuoted to the cold sinceritie of imaginarie constancie, I leaue you to be as you may, and purpose my selfe to be as I list: Neuertheles, to your Maiestie, by whom I haue obtained this libertie, in token of my thankfulnes, I offer this simple work of mine owne hands, which you may weare as you please, but I made it after mine owne minde to be worne loose.

Const. And I who by your comming am not onely set at libertie, but made partaker also of constancie, doe present you with as vnworthie a worke of mine owne hands, which yet I hope you will better accept, bicause it will serue to binde the loosnes of that inconstant dames token.

Inconst. To binde the loosnes, and that of an inconstant dame, say no more than you know, for you knowe not so much as I feele; well may we bewray our selues betweene our selues, as thinking we haue said nothing, vntill we haue saide all. But now, a greater power worketh in me, than your or my reason, which draweth me from the circle of my fancies, to the center of constant loue, there representing vnto me what contentment it is, to loue but one, and how desire is satisfied with no number, when once it delighteth in more than one.

Const. I am not, I cannot be as I was, the leaue that I did take of my selfe, is to leaue my selfe, and to change, or rather to be changed to that estate which admitteth no change: by the secret power of hir, which though she were content to let me be caried almost out of breath with the winde of inconstancie, doth now in hir silence put me to silence, and by the glorie of hir countenance, which disperseth the flying cloudes of vaine conceites, commands me too with others, and to be my selfe as she is, *Semper eadem.*

The Preamble to N.B. his Garden plot.

SWeete fellow whom I sware, such sure affected loue,
As neither weale, nor woe, nor want, can from my minde remoue:
To thee my fellow sweete, this wofull tale I tell,
To let thee see the darke distresse, wherein my minde doth dwel.

On loathed bed I lay, my lustlesse lims to rest,
Where still I tumble to and fro, to seeke which side were best:
At last I catch a place, where long I cannot lie,
But strange conceits from quiet sleepes, do keep awake mine eie.

The time of yeere me seemes, doth bid me slouen rise,
And not from shew of sweete delight, to shut my sleepie eies:
But sorrow by and by, doth bid me slaue lie still,
And slug amongst the wretched souls, whom care doth seek to kil.

   For sorow is my spring, which brings forth bitter teares,
   The fruits of friendship all forlorne, as feeble fancie feares.

A strange description of a rare Garden plot,
Written by N.B. Gent.

MY garden ground of griefe: where selfe wils seeds are sowne,
Whereof comes vp the weedes of wo, that ioies haue
ouergrown:
With patience paled round, to keep in secret spight:
And quickset round about with care, to keepe out all delight.

Foure quarters squared out, I finde in sundrie sort;
Whereof according to their kindes, I meane to make report:
The first, the knot of loue, drawne euen by true desier,
Like as it were two harts in one, and yet both would be nier.

The herbe is calde Isop, the iuice of such a taste,
As with the sowre, makes sweete conceits to flie away too fast:
The borders round about, are set with priuie sweete,
Where neuer bird but nightingale, presumde to set hir feete.

From this I stept aside, vnto the knot of care,
Which so was crost with strange conceits, as tong cannot declare:
The herbe was called Time, which set out all that knot:
And like a Maze me thought it was, when in the crookes I got.

The borders round about, are Sauerie vnsweete:
An herbe not much in my conceit, for such a knot vnmeete:
From this to friendships knot, I stept and tooke the view,
How it was drawne, and then againe, in order how it grew.

The course was not vnlike, a kinde of hand in hand:
But many fingers were away, that there should seeme to stand:
The herbe that set the knot, was Pennie Riall round:
And as me seem'd, it grew full close, and nere vnto the ground.

And parched heere and there, so that it seemed not
Full as it should haue been in deed, a perfect friendship knot:
Heerat I pawsd awhile, and tooke a little view
Of an od quarter drawne in beds, where herbs and flowers grew.

The flowres were buttons fine, for batchelers to beare,
And by those flowres ther grew an herb, was called maiden hear.

Amid this garden ground, a Condit strange I found,
Which water fetcht from sorows spring, to water al the ground:
To this my heauie house, the dungeon of distresse,
Where fainting hart lies panting still, despairing of redresse.

Whence from my window loe, this sad prospect I haue,
A piece of ground wheron to gaze, would bring one to his graue:
Lo thus the welcome spring, that others lends delight,
Doth make me die, to thinke I lie, thus drowned in despight,

That vp I cannot rise, and come abrode to thee,
My fellow sweet, with whom God knowes, how oft I wish to bee:
And thus in haste adieu, my hart is growne so sore,
And care so crookes my fingers ends, that I can write no more.

An excellent Dreame of Ladies and
their Riddles: by N.B. Gent.

IN Orchard grounds, where store of fruit trees grew,
  Me thought a Saint was walking all alone,
  Of euerie tree, she seemd to take hir view,
But in the end, she plucked but of one:
    This fruit quoth she, doth like my fancie best:
    Sweetings are fruit, but let that apple rest.

Such fruit (quoth I) shall fancie chiefly feede:
Indeede tis faire, God grant it prooue as good,
But take good heede, least all to late it breede
Ill humors such as may infect your blood:
    Yet take and taste, but looke you know the tree:
    Peace foole quoth she, and so awaked mee.

What was this ground, wherein this dame did walke?

And what was she, that romed to and fro?
And what ment I, to vse such kinde of talke?
And what ment she, to checke and snib me so?
    But what meane I? alas, I was asleepe:
    Awake I sweare, I will more silence keepe.

Well thus I wakte and fell asleepe againe:
And then I fell into another vaine.
Great wars me thought grew late by strange mishap,
Desire had stolne out of Dianaes traine,
Hir darling deere, and laid on Venus lap,
Who, Cupid sware should neuer backe againe.
    Ere he would so loose all his harts delight,
    He vow'd to die, wherewith began a fight.

Diana shot, and Cupid shot againe:
Fame sounded out hir trumpe with heauenly cheare:
Hope was ill hurt, despite was onely slaine:
Diana forst in fine for to retire.
    Cupid caught fame, and brought hir to his frend:
    The trumpet ceast, and so my dreame did end.

Thus scarce awake, I fell asleepe againe,
And then I was within a garden ground,
Beset with flowres, the allies euen and plaine:
And all the banks beset with roses round.
    And sundrie flowres so super sweete of smell,
    As there me thought it was a heauen to dwell.

Where walking long, anon I gan espie
Sweete pretie soules, that pluckt ech one a flowre:
When from their sight I hid me by and by,
Behinde a banke within a brier bowre:
    Where after walke, I saw them where they sat:
    Beheld their hues, and heard their pretie chat:

Sister quoth one, how shall we spend this day?
Deuise (quoth she) some pretie merie iest:
Content quoth one, beshrew them that say nay:

Some purposes or riddles I thinke best:
>Riddles cried all, and so the sport begun:
>Forfet a fillop, she that first hath done.

Loe thus a while was curtsey to propound,
Yet in the end this order did they take,
By two and two, they should sit close and round;
And one begin, another answere make:
>Whose ridling sports in order as I can,
>I will recite, and thus the first began.

The first Riddle.

Within a gallant plot of ground,
There growes a flowre that hath no name,
The like whereof was neuer found,
And none but one can plucke the same:
>Now where this ground or flowre doth growe,
>Or who that one, tis hard to knowe.

The Answere.

Sister (quoth she) if thou wouldst knowe
This ground, this flowre, and happie man,
Walke in this garden to and fro:
Here you shall see them now and than:
>Which when you finde to your delight,
>Then thinke I hit your riddle right.

The Second Riddle.

Within a field there growes a flowre,
That decks the ground where as it growes,
It springs and falls, both in an howre,
And but at certaine times it showes:
>It neuer dies, and seldome seene,
>And tis a Nosegay for a Queene.

The Answere.

This field is fauor, Grace the ground,
Whence springs the flowre of curtesie,
Soone growne and gone though somtime found,
Not dead, but hid, from flattrers eie,
    That pickthanks may not plucke the same:
    Thus haue I red your riddle Dame.

The third Riddle.

Within a flowre a seede there growes,
Which somtime falls, but seldome springs,
And if it spring, it seldome blowes,
And if it blowe, no sweete it brings,
    And therefore counted but a weede:
    Now gesse the flowre, and what the seede.

The Answere.

In fancies flowre is sorrowes seede,
Which somtimes falls, but springs but seeld,
And if it spring, tis but a weede,
Which doth no sweete, nor sauor yeeld,
    And yet the flowre, both faire and sweete,
    And for a Princes garden meete.

The fourth Riddle.

Within a seede doth poison lurke,
Which onely Spiders feede vpon,
And yet the Bee can wisely woorke,
To sucke out honie, poison gone:
    Which honie, poison, Spider, Bee,
    Are hard to gesse, yet eath to see.

The Answere.

In sorrowes seede is secret paine,

Which spite the Spider onely sucks,
Which poison gone, then wittie braine
The wilie Bee, hir honie plucks,
    And beares it to hir hiue vnhurt,
    When spider trod, dies in the durt.

Gramercie wench (quoth she) that first begoon,
Each one me seemes hath quit hir selfe right well,
And now since that our riddles all are doon,
Let vs go sing the flowre of sweetest smell:
    Well may it fare, wherewith each tooke a part,
    And thus they soong, all with a merie hart.

Blest be the ground that first brought forth the flowre,
Whose name vntolde, but vertues not vnknowne:
Happie the hand, whom God shall giue the powre,
To plucke this flowre, and take it for his owne:
    Oh heauenly stalke, that staines all where it growes:
    From whom more sweet, than sweetest hony flowes.

Oh sweete of sweetes, the sweetest sweete that is:
Oh flowre of flowres, that yeelds so sweete a sent:
Oh sent so sweete, as when the head shall misse:
Oh heauens what hart but that will sore lament:
    God let thee spring, and flourish so each howre,
    As that our sweetes may neuer turne to sowre.

For we with sweetes doe seede our fancies so,
With sweetes of sight, and sweetnes of conceit,
That we may wish that it may euer groe,
Amid delights where we desire to wait,
    Vpon the flowre that pleaseth euerie eie,
    And glads each hart; God let it neuer die.

Wherewith me thought alowd I cride, Amen:
And therewithall I started out of sleepe:
Now what became of these faire Ladies then,
I cannot tell, in minde I onely keepe
    These ridling toies which heere I doe recite:
    Ile tell ye more perhaps another night.

The Chesse Play.
Very aptly deuised by N.B. Gent.

A Secret many yeeres vnseene,
In play at Chesse, who knowes the game,
First of the King, and then the Queene,
Knight, Bishop, Rooke, and so by name,
    Of euerie Pawne I will descrie,
    The nature with the qualitie.

The King.

The King himselfe is haughtie Care,
Which ouerlooketh all his men,
And when he seeth how they fare,
He steps among them now and then,
    Whom, when his foe presumes to checke,
    His seruants stand, to giue the necke.

The Queene.

The Queene is queint, and quicke Conceit,
Which makes hir walke which way she list,
And rootes them vp, that lie in wait
To worke hir treason, ere she wist:
    Hir force is such against hir foes,
    That whom she meetes, she ouerthrowes.

The Knight.

The Knight is knowledge how to fight
Against his Princes enimies,
He neuer makes his walke outright,
But leaps and skips, in wilie wise,
    To take by sleight a traitrous foe,
    Might slilie seeke their ouerthrowe.

The Bishop.

The Bishop he is wittie braine,
That chooseth Crossest pathes to pace,
And euermore he pries with paine,
To see who seekes him most disgrace:
    Such straglers when he findes astraie,
    He takes them vp, and throwes awaie.

The Rookes.

The Rookes are reason on both sides,
Which keepe the corner houses still,
And warily stand to watch their tides,
By secret art to worke their will,
    To take sometime a theefe vnseene,
    Might mischiefe meane to King or Queene.

The Pawnes.

The Pawne before the king, is peace,
Which he desires to keepe at home,
Practise, the Queenes, which doth not cease
Amid the world abroad to roame,
    To finde, and fall vpon each foe,
    Whereas his mistres meanes to goe.

Before the knight, is perill plast,
Which he, by skipping ouergoes,
And yet that Pawne can worke a cast,
To ouerthrow his greatest foes;
    The Bishops, prudence, prieng still,
    Which way to worke his masters will.

The Rookes poore Pawnes, are sillie swaines,
Which seeldome serue, except by hap,
And yet those Pawnes, can lay their traines,
To catch a great man, in a trap:
    So that I see, sometime a groome
    May not be spared from his roome.

The nature of the Chesse men.

The King is stately, looking hie;
The Queene, doth beare like maiestie:
The Knight, is hardie, valiant, wise:
The Bishop, prudent, and precise:
    The Rookes, no raungers out of raie,
    The Pawnes, the pages in the plaie.

L ENV OY.

Then rule with care, and quicke conceit,
And fight with knowledge, as with force;
So beare a braine, to dash deceit,
And worke with reason and remorse:
    Forgiue a fault, when yoong men plaie,
    So giue a mate, and go your way.

And when you plaie beware of Checke,
Know how to saue and giue a necke:
And with a Checke, beware of Mate;
But cheefe, ware had I wist too late:
    Loose not the *Queene,* for ten to one,
    If she be lost, the game is gone.

A most rare, and excellent Dreame, lear-
nedly set downe by a woorthy Gentleman,
a braue Scholler, and M. of Artes
in both Vniuersities.

THe while we sleepe, whereof may it proceed,
    Our minde is led with dreames of diuers sorts,
    Some fearfull things, and discontentment breede,
Some merriment, and pretie idle sports,
And some of future things presage imports;
    Some wounds the conscience with the former gilt,
    Of outrage, wrongs, and bloud vniustly spilt.

Some strange effects if not impossible,
As to be caried in the emptie aire,
Of transformations some incredible,
From forme to forme, and of their backe repaire,
Some pleasant shewes presents, and some dispaire:
    Some grauer things a sleeping can discusse:
    And other, matters meere ridiculous.

Men diuersly do argue of the cause
Of dreames: Some their occasion thus recites,
The while the bodie takes his needfull pause,
In sleepe to fresh and to restore the sprites,
Decaid by labor, or the daies delites,
    The minde, the cogitations of the day do keepe,
    And run them ouer when we are asleepe.

Others our meates do charge with those effects
That indigested in the stomacke lies:
Other celestiall influence respects,
And fetch from them our sleeping fantasies;
The which they recommend as Prophesies:
    For when our sprites are stirred with those charms,
    We are foretold of good or future harms.

But this coniecture cheefly I embrace,
Euen as the sea enraged with the winde,
After the storme alaid will mooue a space,
The selfe same reason may be well assignde,
Vnto the nightly labors of the minde:
    Who works in sleepe, our actions at a stay,
    Vpon th'occasions of the passed day.

Vpon a dreame I had, I this prefer,
The which the sequell shall deliuer straite:
That Loue that first did make my reason erre,
Straitly one day commanded me to waite,
On paine to pine, and perish in conceite;
    Vpon my soueraigne, vnto whom I went,
    As dutie wild, and Loues commandement.

Mine eies, the first intreating messengers,
By signes of sorrow openly did speake,
After my toong the humble suite prefers
Of my poore hart, with torments like to breake:
But little of my suffrings doth she reake:
    Sooner the rocks their hardnes will forgo,
    Than she acknowledge that which she doth know.

In fine, vnto my chamber I retire,
A thousand fancies hamring on my wits,
Despaire, griefe, anguish, furie, and desire,
Doe exercise in turne their Bedlem fits,
Whereof to speake, or heare, best them befits,
    That now enioyeng, heretofore haue tride,
    The hell, and bitternes of Loue denide.

By this the night doth through the skie display
Hir sable robe, spangled with golden stars,
And voicelesse silence gan to chace away
Noyses and sounds, with their molesting iars:
And so the place to needfull sleepe prepars;
    Who Motherlike, most tenderly asswages,
    The daies aggreeuances and damages.

Encumbred thus, I went vnto my bed,
Loue knowes, with litle hope of taking rest,
Fancie and frenzie worketh on my head,
One while the one, then th'other gets the best:
Now eithers faction egarly addrest;
    To hostile conflict furiously discend,
    Of purpose strait to make a finall end.

Extremitie proceeding on so far,
When eithers forces equally were spent,
They stinted of themselues this raging war,
And left with victorie indifferent:
Slumber that found the time conuenient,
    Seeing the slacknes of their wearied traine,
    Vpon th'aduantage seased on my braine.

Who holding me vnder his shadie wings,
To mitigate the anguish of my thought,
Presented me with diuers pleasant things,
Amongst the rest, a Ladie faire he brought,
From heauen no doubt those features there are wrought,
    Whose raies of beautie admirable bright,
    Filled my chamber with a Sunshine light.

Hir Amber tresses on hir shoulders lies,
The which as she doth moue, diuided run,
About hir bodie iust in circle wise,
Like to the curious web Arachne spun;
Or else to make a fit comparison,
    Like slender twist turned to shining fire,
    Or flames by woonder wrought into a wire.

The forehead that confines these burnisht haires,
For whitenes striueth with vntouched snowe;
For smoothnes with the Iuorie compares;
And doth the Alablasters glistring showe,
Vnder this firmament you are to know,
    Two powrfull stars which at their pleasure moue,
    The variable effects that followes loue.

Hir cheekes resembleth right a garden plot,
Of diuers sorts of rare Carnation flowres,
The which the scortching Sun offendeth not,
Nor boystrous winter with his rotting showres;
Vncertaine Iuno thereon neuer lowres:
    Heere Venus with hir little loues reposes,
    Amongst the lillies and the damaske roses.

Hir lips compares with the Vermilion morne,
Hir equall teeth in semicircle wise,
For orientnes selected pearle may scorne,
What may I of hir issuing breath deuise,
That from this pearle and Synaber doth rise:
    The francumsence and myrr, that Inde presents,
    Within this aire leese their extolled sents.

The nose, the chin, the straight erected necke,
Supporter to the head: next shoulders stands,
The which discends into the arme direct,
And terminates their length vpon the hands:
At each of these my wits amased stands:
    For when I would their merits vtter foorth,
    I finde all words inferior to their woorth.

The garments wherewithall she was attyrde,
But slender in account, and yet were more
Than hir perfections needfully requyrde,
Whose euery part hath of contentment store:
But as it was, thanks to my dreame therefore,
    Who causde the apparition to be wrought,
    As all lay open to mine eies or thought.

There was, as I obseru'd next to hir skin,
A snowe white lawne, transparent as the aire,
And ouer this a garment wondrous thin,
Of networke, wrought in blacke, exceeding faire;
Whose masks were small, and thred as fine as haire,
    Girt with a tawnie Cyprous were hir clothes,
    And thus attirde, this Angell woman goes.

Hir mouing brests as equall Promontories,
Diuided by an Indraft from the maine,
Doe imitate the gently moued Seas,
That rising fall, and falling rise againe:
As they, so did my life in euery vaine:
    My spirit issued as they waxed hier,
    And as they setled, backe againe retier.

Next neighbor heerunto in due discent,
Hir bellie plaine, the bed of namelesse blisse,
Wherein all things appeere aboue content,
And paradise is nothing more than this:
In which Desire was mou'd to doe amisse;
    For when his eies vpon this tree was cast,
    O blame him not, if he requirde to taste.

What followed this, I cannot well report:
The tawnie Cyprous that forehanging fell,
Restraind mine eies in most malitious sort,
Which of themselues were else affected well,
Although as witnes nought thereof I tell:
 I doubt not those that fine conceited be,
 Sees somwhat further, than mine eies might see.

But of hir praises thus in generall,
Desirde perfection shewd in euerie part,
Yet all appeerd in each one seuerall,
Vnto the wonder of the eie and hart,
Of euery priuate part to write apart.
 Were worke and argument for him that vses,
 The daily conuersation of the Muses.

Who this should be, if any long to heare,
I say it is the portraict of the Saint,
Which deepe ingraued in my hart I beare,
The Mistres of my hope, my feare, and plaint,
And thou that with hir praises I acquaint,
 If thou canst nothing else, yet wish thou me,
 Deliuerd of that beauties crueltie.

With vnperceiued motion drawing ny,
Vnto the bed of my distresse and feare,
She with hir hand doth put the curtaine by,
And sits hir downe vpon the one side there:
My wasted spirits quite amazed were,
 To see the sudden morning of those eies,
 Within the darke thus inexpected rise.

Being abrode (quoth she) I lately hard,
That you were falne into a sudden feuer,
And solitarie in your chamber bard,
From companie you did your selfe disseuer,
To charitie it appertaineth euer,
 In duties to our neighbors for to sticke,
 And visit the afflicted and the sicke.

Which Christian office hither hath me led,
Wishing I could recouerie to you bring,
Ladie (quoth I) as easily done as sed,
For you that haue my life in managing,
What need you wish, when you may doe the thing:
    For if you be disposd to charitie,
    Bestowe on me this wisht recouerie.

Is't in my garden that may doe thee good?
(Quoth she) or in my closet of conserues,
Or may my kitchin any kinde of foode
Deuise, that to thy taste and fancie serues,
Ladie (said I) no coolice, no conserues,
    No herbe, no potion commeth nie that part,
    That suffereth this anguish and this smart.

When further I would faine haue spoken on,
With fearfulnes I felt my toong restrained,
And shamefastnes with red Vermilion,
My shallow cheekes and countenance distained:
Now by this meanes my hart more deepely pained,
    Sent out a flood of weeping to betoken,
    The rest of that my toong had left vnspoken.

As soone as sighes had ouerblowne my teares,
And teares allaid my sighings vehemence,
Audacitie expulser of those feares,
Gaue to desire at last preheminence,
Who saw it now to be of consequence;
    Sauced his tale with dutie and respect,
    And thus began, or to the like effect.

It is no feuer (Ladie) in the vaines,
Nor in the blood, of humors the excesse,
Nor stomacks vapor, that annoies the braines,
Nor ill contagion in the Arteries,
Nor any griefe that Physicke remedies:
    It is, &c. and heere my lips refusde to moue,
    Stopping the sentence ere I came to Loue.

Haply (said she) as I doe iudge thereon,
It is some toy or fancie in your head,
Some sicknes grounded on opinion,
Or else some error your conceit hath bred:
Then as suppose you to this anguish led,
 By mine aduice, if you list ruled be,
 For health sake doe suppose the contrarie.

Were it within the compas of my wits,
(Leader of my desires) thus I replide,
To remedie the outrage of those fits,
That from this bodie would my life diuide,
The rather should these cordials be applide,
 That I might keepe my life in health, to doe,
 The seruices that loue commands me to.

But out alas, that waied downe with paine,
With hands erected vp, that I should crie,
As doth the saylers blowne into the maine,
After the ship that fore the winde doth flie,
And yet in sight of helpe, must helpeles die:
 So I, neere hir that can my woes appease,
 Doe perish like the outcast in the Seas.

Are you the woorser that I am so neere,
The Ladie said, and I not thereof ware?
Nay happie then (quoth I) that you are heere,
And haples too, bicause you are so farre:
She aunswered hereunto, these riddles are:
 Can neere be far, can happy haples be?
 As well (quoth I) as see, and not to see.

What is he (Madame) that doth baite his eies,
Be he of mortall or immortall kinde,
Vpon the beauties which your visage dies,
And drawes not present death into his minde,
Vnles your gratious lookes do prooue so kinde,
 As with a yeelding fauour to preuent,
 The dangers thereunto are incident.

Can it be possible you should not knowe
The powre and vertue of sweete beauties gift?
Can heauen and nature measureles bestowe
The things that you to Angels calling lift?
And you not vnderstand their purpos'd drift?
    Might they aduance yee to a Goddesse seate
    And you be ignorant why they make yee great?

If this were true, which you of me suppose,
The praise of beautie, and commended parts,
I see no reason to esteeme of those,
That do complaine them of such pettie smarts,
Not incident to men of valiant harts:
    The argument is dull, and nothing quicke,
    Bicause that I am faire, you should be sicke.

Suppose I haue those graces and those flowres,
And all the vertues that you can recite,
You looke, you like, and you must haue them yours;
Forsooth, bicause they mooue your appetite:
I see no reason to impart my right,
    Before that God and men agreed be,
    To let all things run in communitie.

An easie thing for you to ouercome,
(Faire Ladie) him, that is so deepe your thrall:
For euery syllable from your lips that come,
Beares wit, and weight, and vehemence withall:
Vnder the which, my subiect spirits fall:
    If you do speake, or if you nought expresse,
    Your beautie of it selfe is Conqueresse.

With fauour (Ladie) giue me leaue to speake,
(If you will listen a condemneds tale)
No pettie wound can make my hart strings breake:
Nor might a trifle worke this deadly bale:
Your soueraigne beautie doth me hither hale:
    The stronger doth (euen by a common course)
    Ouer the weaker exercise his force.

Ladie, in condiscending vnto Loue,
You do not share nor yet your right forgo,
In that you shall your seruants sute approue,
And blesse him with those fauors you can showe,
To higher place of dignitie you growe:
    The Sun were not in my opinion bright,
    If there were not eie witnes of his light.

No abiect commons of those things he seekes,
Nor any way doth labor to induce
That liues to serue and honor hir he leekes,
In hope at last to make an happie truce,
And for this cause all other he refuse:
    To exercise those parts with serious care,
    Which to his Mistres fancie pleasing are.

But sir (quoth she) how can ye answere this?
You men complaine, Loues torments to be great;
Saying that he a mightie Tyrant is;
Such one as putteth reason from hir seat;
Why wish ye to insnare me in this net?
    Better it is you suffer that you doe,
    Then such extreames should happen vpon two.

When Loue (sweete Ladie) thorowly accords,
The Louers and beloueds harts in one,
This amitie a perfect heauen affords,
Vpon the instant of this vnion:
Banisht is thence all sorrow, care, and mone,
    For they which in conspiring Loue abide,
    Liue with continuall ioies, vnsatisfide.

This is beleeu'd and knowne by common brute,
When of vs Dames ye hap to get a graunt,
You giue it to the cunning of your sute,
Vsing with your companions thus to vaunt:
These pretie fooles, tis nothing to enchaunt:
    As fishers vse for fish, with fish to bait,
    These faire ones, so, faire speeches catches strait.

Let not (sweete Loue) the fault of one or few,
Or sinister report of truthelesse fame,
Endamage the desart of him can shew
Many effects repugnant to the same,
Vnworthie he of life, or Louers name,
    Shall dare vnto hir honor, wrong, or scathe,
    Of whom both life, and happines he hathe.

It is a proofe (said she) of foolishnes,
To set that vpon chaunce which may be sure,
Exempt from Loue, I liue in happines,
In which condition I will yet indure:
Griefes come apace, we neede not them procure:
    In the estate I liue, I am content,
    And minde not Loue, in dread of discontent.

I know (quoth I) you can from Loue refraine,
Bicause he holds his state within your eies:
But I, the vassall of his hard disdaine,
Am so deiected, as I cannot rise;
Albeit my sute and seruice you dispise,
    Yet giue me leaue to honor and admire,
    Your beautie which afflicteth my desire.

Ther's little reason (said she then) to like
The thing which you affirme to vexe ye so,
If your desire such discontentment strike,
Such war, such anguish, agonies, and woe,
Let that fantastike I aduise ye goe:
    The man is much desirous of vnrest,
    That home intreates a knowne disquiet guest.

Excepting Loue, demaund you at my hand,
What euer is in my abilitie:
And may with vertue, and mine honor stand,
Ladie (said I) Loue is the Maladie,
And vnto Loue, Loue's th'onely remedie:
    But sith you doe herein my sute detest,
    Then grant me this, the last I shall request.

When haples Loue hath brought me to the graue,
If so at any time you passe that way,
Where my consuming bones their buriall haue,
Vouchsafe yee then for pitties sake to say,
As I remember, heere my seruant lay,
    Long time a Louer in affection true,
    Whom my disdaine and rigor ouerthrew.

Altho yee die (quoth she) I will not loue,
And for you will not loue (said I) I die:
Then presently my spirits faild to moue,
Retiring backe themselues successiuelie:
But when she did the signe of death espie,
    She puld, she halde, seruant (said she) abide,
    Let not thy mistres be thy homicide.

If thy affections doe from Loue proceede,
How canst thou die, and I thy liues life neere?
If thou doost loue, and honor me indeede,
Why with this act dost thou defame me heere?
If thou esteemst my Loue and honor deere,
    O liue, and see my rigour ouerthrowne,
    And come and take possession of thine owne.

And then vnable weeping to withholde,
She sundrie meanes assaies to make me liue,
My brests she strikes, she rubs my temples colde,
And with such vehemence of labours striue,
As life vnto a Marble stone might giue:
    My hand at last, she amorously doth straine,
    And with a kisse drew vp my life againe.

This new sprong ioy conceiued in my hart,
Of Loues assurance vnder hand and seale,
Dilated thence abroad to euery part,
Telling how graciouslie my loue did deale,
My soule and spirit swelling with this zeale,
    So rowsed sleepe, that he his holde forsooke,
    And I through surfeit of the ioy awooke.

Awaked thus, I presently perceiu'd,
The vanitie and falshood of these ioyes;
Finding that fond illusions had deceiu'd
My ouerwatched braine with idle toyes;
Then I that freshly felt my first annoyes,
    Their woonted rage within my thoughts to keepe,
    Gan thus expostulate the cause with sleepe.

Thou ease of harts, with burth'nous woes opprest,
Thou pitier of the cares of busie daie,
Thou friend to louers in their deepe vnrest,
Turning their anguishes another waie,
Why may not I continue with thee aie,
    Sith that my destinie is so extreame,
    As not to haue my good, but in a dreame.

Why art thou not (O dreame) the same you seeme?
Seeing thy visions our contentment brings;
Or doe we of their woorthines misdeeme?
To call them shadowes that are reall things?
And falslie attribute their due to wakings?
    O doe but then perpetuate thy sleight,
    And I will sweare, thou workst not by deceit.

And now the Morning entring at the glasse,
Made of these thoughts some intermission:
Thus haue I tolde what things in dreame did passe,
Vpon the former daies occasion;
And whence they come in mine opinion;
    But whether they tell truth, or nothing lesse,
    I shall resolue, vpon my dreames successe.

Excellent Ditties of diuers kindes, and
rare inuention: written by
sundry Gentlemen.

WEepe you my lines for sorrow whilst I write
    For you alone may manifest my griefe,
    Your numbers must my endles woes recite,
Such woes as wound my soule without reliefe,
    Such bitter woes, as who so would disclose them,
    Must cease to talke, for hart can scarse suppose them.

My restles braines deuour'd by many thoughts,
Disclaiming ioies doth make a heauen of hell,
An Idoll of mislikes, a God of noughts,
Contrarious passions on my braine doth dwell,
    They would haue ease, yet seeke for ceaslesse strife,
    And make their cause of death, their meanes of life.

Mine eies are dim'd by two diuine delights,
And through their sight, my hart hath caught a wound:
Their lids were shut amids the lingring nights:
Their yeelding fountaines watring of the ground,
    Doe ceasles run, and shroud their shining ioy,
    And drowne Content in riuers of annoy.

I faine to smile, when as I faint for feare:
I dreame on ioy, when as I doubt of woe:
I burne in fire, yet still approch it neare:
I like of mirth, yet will no solace knowe:
    I see content, yet neuer cease to sigh:
    I liue secure, yet danger passeth nigh.

I catch at hope, yet ouertake it neuer:
I feede on thought, yet thought doth force my end:
I craue repose, yet finde disquiet euer:
I scorne aduice, yet counsell is my frend:
    I will be free, yet feede on thraldome still:
    I honor wit, yet feede on foolish will.

Mine eies complaine the follies of my hart:
My hart laments the errors of mine eie:
My thoughts would burie endles things in art:
Mine eie, my hart, my thoughts, wend all awrie:
    Yet of my harmes (ye heauens) the worst is this;
    I cannot censure what my sorrow is.

My life is death, for no delights are in it:
My musike mone, and yet I neuer leaue it:
My succour hope, yet can I neuer win it:
My gaines report, yet will I not perceiue it:
    My foode suspect, and yet I cannot flie it:
    My foe neglect, and yet I meane to trie it.

By day I freeze, I frie, I wish, I wait:
By night I loath my rest, and wish for day:
Both day and night, my hart with doubts I bait:
Weying delight from cause of my decaie:
    The Vultures that consume my tender brest,
    Is sweete desire, the cause of my vnrest.

Now what I am, my sorie cheekes disclose:
Once what I was, my smiling eies bewraid:
Now what I want, coniecture by my woes:
Once what I scornd, hath now my hart betraid:
    Wo's me, my want of helpe doth well approue,
    The paines I feele, is euen the pangs of Loue.

Well, be it paine, Loues torments let it be:
Let endles thoughts consume my restles braines:
Let teares so choake mine eies, I may not see:
Let toong be mute, for to disclose my paines:
    Let ioyes, let hope, let all contents surcease,
    These bitter plagues, my fancies shall increase.

No paine, no fortune shall my Loue confound:
My spotles faith, my simple truth shall proue,
That I my liking on no errors ground:
Thus will I liue, thus will I passe my Loue:

    Repulse, contempt, can neuer alter kinde;
    Loues triumph doth consist in constant minde.

With constant minde the poore remainder gift,
That Loue amongst his many spoyles hath left me,
Is that which to the heauens my face shall lift,
Though other hope by fortune be bereft me;
    And if I die, this praise shall me await,
    My Loue was endlesse, voide of all deceit.

FINIS

Vses helpe me, sorrow swarmeth,
Eies are fraught with seas of languish,
Haples hope my solace harmeth:
Mindes repast is bitter anguish.

Eie of daie regarded neuer,
Certaine trust in world vntrustie,
Flattring hope beguileth euer:
Wearie olde, and wanton lustie.

Dawne of day, beholdes inthroned,
Fortunes darling proud and dreadles:
Darksome night doth heare him moned,
Who before was rich and needles.

Rob the spheare of lines vnited;
Make a sudden voide in nature:
Force the day to be benighted;
Reaue the cause of time, and creature.

Ere the world will cease to varie:
This I weepe for, this I sorrow:
Muses if you please to tarie,
Further helpe I meane to borrow.

Courted once by fortunes fauor,
Compast now with enuies curses:
All my thoughts of sorrowes sauor,
Hopes run fleeting like the Sourses.

Ay me wanton scorne hath maimed
All the ioies my hart enioied:
Thoughts their thinking haue disclaimed,
Hate my hopes haue quite annoied.

Scant regard my weale hath scanted:
Looking coie hath forst my lowring:
Nothing likte, where nothing wanted,
Weds mine eies to ceasles showring.

Former Loue was once admired,
Present fauor is estranged:
Loath'd the pleasure long desired;
Thus both men and thoughts are changed.

Louely Swaine with luckie speeding,
Once (but now no more) so frended:
Thou my flocks hast had in feeding,
From the morne, till day was ended.

Drinke and fodder, foode and folding,
Had my lambes and ewes togeather:
I with them was still beholding,
Both in warmth, and winter weather.

Now they languish since refused,
Ewes and lambes are paind with pining:
I with ewes and lambes confused,
All vnto our deathes declining.

Silence leaue thy caue obscured,
Daine a dolefull Swaine to tender,
Though disdaines I haue endured,
Yet I am no deepe offender.

Philips sonne can with his finger,
Hide his scar, it is so little:
Little sinne a day to linger,
Wise men wander in a tittle.

Trifles yet my Swaine haue turned,
Tho my sonne he neuer showeth:
Tho I weepe, I am not mourned,
Tho I want, no pitie groweth.

Yet for pitie loue my muses,
Gentle silence be their couer,
They must leaue their wonted vses,
Since I leaue to be a Louer.

They shall liue with thee inclosed,
I will loath my pen and paper:
Art shall neuer be supposed,
Sloth shall quench the watching taper.

Kisse them silence, kisse them kindely,
Tho I leaue them, yet I loue them:
Tho my wit haue led them blindely,
Yet my Swaine did once approue them.

I will trauell soiles remoued,
Night and morning neuer merie,
Thou shalt harbor that I loued,
I will loue that makes me wearie.

If perchaunce the Shepherd straieth,
In thy walks and shades vnhaunted,
Tell the Teene my hart betraieth,
How neglect my ioyes haue daunted.

T. L. Gent.

STriue no more,
  Forspoken ioyes to spring:
Since care hath clipt thy wing:
    But stoope those lampes before:
That nurst thee vp at first, with friendly smiles,
And now through scornes thy trust beguiles.

    Pine away,
That pining you may please;
For death betides you ease:
    Oh sweete and kinde decay;
To pine and die, whilst Loue giues looking on,
And pines to see your pining mone.

    Dying ioyes,
Your shrine is constant hart,
That glories in his smart:
    Your Tropheis are annoyes,
And on your tombe, by Loue these lines are plaste,
Loe heere they lie, whom scorne defaste.

T. L. Gent.

OF ceasles thoughts my mind hath fram'd his wings,
  Wherewith he soares and climes aboue conceit,
And midst his flight for endles ioy he sings,
To spie those double lampes, whose sweete receit
    Must be the heauen where as my soule shall rest,
    Though by their shine my bodie be deprest.

Hir eies shrowd pitie, pietie, and pure,
Hir face shields Roses, Lillies, and delight,
Hir hand hath powre, to conquere and allure,
Hir hart, holds honor, loue, remorce, and right,
    Hir minde is fraught, with wisdome, faith, and loue,
    All what is hirs, is borrowed from aboue.

Then mount my minde, and feare no future fall,
Exceed conceit, for she exceeds conceit:
Burne louely lamps, to whom my lookes are thrall,
My soule shall glorie in so sweete receit,
    Tho in your flames my corse to cinders wend,
    Yet am I proud to gaine a Phœnix end.

T. L. Gent.

WHen Pirrha made hir miracle of stones,
    The baser sort of flintie molde she fram'd,
Whose course compact concealed all at once,
All what in nature could imperfect be,
    So but imperfect perfect, was the shape,
    And minde euen with the mettall did agree.

The finer formes of Diamonds she made,
    A peereles substance matchles for the molde,
Whence grew such shapes that heauen his pure forsook,
To frame a minde agreeing to the forme,

This by my proofe, I finde for certaine true,
For why my mistres matchles in hir shape,
For bodie faire exceeds my base report,
    For minde, no minde can craue more rare supplies,
    And last I spie the Saphirs in hir eies[.]

T. L. Gent.

ALl day I weepe my wearie woes,
    Then when that night approcheth neere,
And euery one his eies doth close,
And passed paines no more appeere,
        I change my cheere,

And in the weepings of mine eie,
Loue bathes his wings, and from my hart
Drawes fire his furie to supplie,
And on my bones doth whet his dart:
      Oh bitter smart.

My sighes within their clouds obscure,
Would blinde mine eies, they might not see,
Those cruell pleasant lamps that lure:
My reason faine would set me free,
      Which may not be.

The dried strawe will take the fire;
The trained brache will follow game:
The idle thought doth still desire:
Fond will is hardly brought in frame:
      The more my blame.

Thus see I how the stormes doe growe,
And yet the paine I still approoue:
I leaue my weale, I follow woe,
I see the rocke, yet nill remooue:
      Oh flie me Loue:

Then midst the stormes I shall preuent,
And by foresight my troubles cease:
And by my reason shun repent;
Thus shall I ioye, if Loue decrease:
      And liue in peace.

          T. L. Gent.

MY fraile and earthly barke by reasons guide,
  (Which holds the helme, whilst will doth yeld the saile)
By my desires the windes of bad betide,
Hath saild these worldly seas with small auaile,
Vaine obiects serue for dreadfull rocks to quaile,

My brittle boate, from hauen of life that flies,
To haunt the Sea of Mundane miseries.

My soule that drawes impressions from aboue,
And viewes my course, and sees the windes aspire,
Bids reason watch to scape the shoales of Loue,
But lawles will enflamde with endles ire,
Doth steere in poope whilst reason doth retire:
    The storms increase, my barke loues billowes fill;
    Thus are they wrackt, that guide their course by will.

             T. L. Gent.

Midst lasting griefes, to haue but short repose,
In little ease, to feede on loath'd suspect,
Through deepe despite, assured loue to lose,
In shew to like, in substance to neglect:

To laugh an howre, to weepe an age of woe,
From true mishap to gather false delight,
To freeze in feare, in inward hart to glowe:
To read my losse within a ruthles sight:

To seeke my weale, and wot not where it lies,
In hidden fraud, an open wrong to finde,
Of ancient thoughts, new fables to deuise,
Delightfull smiles, but yet a scornfull minde:

    These are the meanes that murder my releefe,
    And end my doubtfull hope with certaine greefe.

             T. L. Gent.

OH woods vnto your walks my bodie hies,
To loose the traitrous bonds of ticing Loue,
  Where trees, where herbes, where flowres,

    Their natiue moisture powres,
From foorth their tender stalks to helpe mine eies,
Yet their vnited teares may nothing moue.

When I beheld the faire adorned tree,
Which lightnings force and winters frosts resists,
    Then Daphnes ill betide,
    And Phebus lawles pride,
Enforce me say euen such my sorrowes be,
For selfe disdaine in Phebes hart consists.

If I behold the flowres by morning teares,
Looke louely sweete, ah then forlorne I crie:
    Sweete showres for Memnon shed,
    All flowres by you are fed:
Whereas my pitious plaint that still appeares,
Yeelds vigor to hir scornes and makes me die.

When I regard the pretie greeffull burd,
With tearfull (yet delightfull) notes complaine,
    I yeeld a tenor with my teares,
    And whilst hir musicke wounds mine eares,
Alas say I, why nill my notes affoord
Such like remorce, who still beweepe my paine.

When I behold vpon the leaueles bow,
The haples bird lament hir Loues depart,
    I drawe hir biding nigh,
    And sitting downe I sigh,
And sighing say alas, that birds auow
A setled faith, where Phebe scornes my smart.

Thus wearie in my walks, and woefull too,
I spend the day forespent with daily griefe:
    Each obiect of distresse,
    My sorrow doth expresse:
I doate on that which doth my hart vndoe,
And honor hir that scornes to yeeld reliefe.

                T. L. Gent.

Accurst be loue and they that trust his traines;
He tastes the fruite, whilst others toyle:
  He brings the lampe, we lend the oyle:
  He sowes distres, we yeeld him soyle:
  He wageth warre, we bide the foyle:

Accurst be Loue, and those that trust his traines:
  He laies the trap, we seeke the snare:
  He threatneth death, we speake him faire:
  He coynes deceits, we foster care:
  He fauoreth pride, we count it rare.

Accurst be Loue, and those that trust his traines,
  He seemeth blinde, yet wounds with Art:
  He vowes content, he paies with smart:
  He sweares reliefe, yet kils the hart:
  He cals for truth, yet scornes desart.
Accurst be loue, and those that trust his traines,
Whose heauen, is hell; whose perfect ioyes, are paines.

T. L. Gent.

Now I finde, thy lookes were fained,
Quickly lost, and quicklie gained:
Softe thy skin, like wooll of Wethers,
Hart vnstable, light as feathers:
Toong vntrustie, subtill sighted:
Wanton will with change delighted,
  Sirene pleasant, foe to reason:
  Cupid plague thee, for this treason.

Of thine eies I made my myrror;
From thy beautie came mine error:
All thy words I counted wittie:
All thy smyles I deemed pittie:
Thy false teares that me agreeued,
Full of all my trust deceiued.
  Sirene pleasant, &c.

Fain'd acceptance when I asked,
Louely words with cunning masked;
Holie vowes, but hart vnholie:
Wretched man my trust was follie:
Lillie white, and pretie wincking,
Solemne vowes, but sorie thinking.
    Sirene pleasant, &c.

Now I see, O seemely cruell,
Others warme them at my fuell:
Wit shall guide me in this durance,
Since in Loue is no assurance:
Change thy pasture, take thy pleasure,
Beautie is a fading treasure,
    Sirene pleasant, &c.

Prime youth lasts not, age will follow,
And make white these tresses yelow:
Wrinckled face, for lookes delightfull,
Shall acquaint the dame despitefull:
And when time shall date thy glorie,
Then too late thou wilt be sorie.
    Sirene pleasant, &c.

        T. L. Gent.

THe fatall starre that at my birthday shined,
  Were it of Ioue, or Venus in hir brightnes,
All sad effects, sowre fruits of loue diuined,
                In my Loues lightnes,

Light was my Loue, that all too light beleeued:
Heauens ruthe to dwell in faire alluring faces,
That loue, that hope, that damned, and repreeued,
                To all disgraces.

Loue that misled, hope that deceiu'd my seeing:
Loue hope no more, mockt with deluding obiect:

Sight full of sorow, that denies the being,
                    Vnto the subiect.

Soul leaue the seat, wher thoughts with endles swelling,
Change into teares and words of no persuasion:
Teares turne to tongs, and spend your tunes in telling,
                    Sorowes inuasion.

Wonder vaine world at beauties proud refusall:
Wonder in vaine at Loues vnkinde deniall,
Why Loue thus loftie is, that doth abuse all:
                    And makes no triall.

Teares, words, and tunes, all signifie my sadnes:
My speechles griefe, looke pale without dissembling:
Sorow sit mute, and tell thy torments madnes,
                    With true harts trembling.

And if pure vowes, or hands heau'd vp to heauen,
May moue the Gods to rue my wretched blindnes,
My plaints shall make my ioyes in measure euen,
                    With hir vnkindnes.

That she whom my true hart hath found so cruell,
Mourning all mirthles may pursue the pleasure,
That scornes hir labors: poore in hir ioyes iewell,
                    And earthly treasure.

                    T. L. Gent.

FAine to content, I bend my selfe to write,
    But what to write, my minde can scarce conceiue:
Your radiant eies craue obiects of delight,
My hart no glad impressions can receiue:
    To write of griefe, is but a tedious thing:
    And wofull men, of woe must needly sing.

To write the truce, the wars, the strife, the peace,
That Loue once wrought in my distempred hart:
Were but to cause my woonted woes encrease,
And yeeld new life to my concealed smart:
    Who tempts the eare with tedious lines of griefe,
    That waits for ioy, complaines without reliefe.

To write what paines supplanteth others ioy,
For-thy is folly in the greatest wit,
Who feeles, may best decipher the annoy,
Who knowes the griefe, but he that tasteth it?
    Who writes of woe, must needes be woe begone,
    And writing feele, and feeling write of mone.

To write the temper of my last desire,
That likes me best, and appertains you most:
You are the Pharos whereto now retire,
My thoughts long wandring in a forren coast,
    In you they liue, to other ioyes they die,
    And liuing draw their foode from your faire eie.

Enforst by Loue, and that effectuall fire,
That springs from you to quicken loiall harts:
I write in part the prime of my desire,
My faith, my feare, that springs from your desarts;
    My faith, whose firmnes neuer shunneth triall,
    My feare, the dread and danger of deniall.

To write in briefe, a legend in a line,
My hart hath vow'd to draw his life from yours;
My lookes haue made a Sunne of your sweete eine,
My soule doth drawe his essence from your powres:
    And what I am, in fortune or in loue,
    All those haue sworne, to serue for your behoue.

My sences sucke their comforts from your sweete,
My inward minde, your outward faire admires;
My hope lies prostrate at your pities feete,
My hart, lookes, soule, sence, minde, and hope desires;

Beleefe, and fauour, in your louely sight,
Els all will cease to liue, and pen to write.

T. L. Gent.

FVll fraught with vnrecomptles sweete,
Of your faire face that stole mine eie,
No gladsome day my lookes did greete,
Wherein I wisht not willingly;
    Mine eies were shut I might not see,
    A Ladie of lesse maiestie.

What most I like, I neuer minde,
And so on you haue fixt my thoughts,
That others sights doe make me blinde,
And what I see but you is noughts;
    By vse and custome thus you see,
    Another nature liues in mee.

The more I looke, the more I loue,
The more I thinke, the more I thriue,
No obiect can my looke remoue,
No thought can better thoughts reuiue,
    For what I see or thinke, I finde,
    Exceedeth sight or thought of minde.

Since then your lookes, haue stolne mine eies,
And eies content to nourish loue,
And loue doth make my thoughts arise,
And thoughts are firme, and will not moue,
    Vouchsafe to knit by powre vnknowne,
    Our eies, our loues, our thoughts in one.

T. L. Gent.

Like desart woods, with darksome shades obscured,
Where dredful beasts, wher hateful horror raigneth
Such is my wounded hart whom sorrow paineth.

The trees, are fatall shafts, to death inured,
That cruell Loue within my breast maintaineth,
To whet my griefe, when as my sorrow waineth.

The gastly beasts, my thoughts in cares assured,
Which wage me warre, whilst hart no succor gaineth,
With false suspect, and feare that still remaineth.

The horrors, burning sighes by cares procured,
Which forth I send, whilst weeping eie complaineth,
To coole the heate, the helples hart containeth.

But shafts, but cares, sighes, horrors vnrecured,
Were nought esteemde, if for these paines awarded,
My faithfull Loue by you might be rewarded.

T L Gent

For pittie pretie eies surcease,
To giue me warre, and graunt me peace,
Triumphant eies, why beare you Armes,
Against a hart that thinks no harmes.
A hart alreadie quite appalde,
A hart that yeelds, and is enthrald,
Kill Rebels prowdly that resist,
Not those that in true faith persist.
And conquered serue your Deitie,
Will you alas commaund me die?
Then die I yours, and death my crosse,
But vnto you pertains the losse.

T. L. Gent.

MY bonie Lasse thine eie,
          So flie,
Hath made me sorrowe so:
Thy Crimsen cheekes my deere,
          So cleere,
Haue so much wrought my woe.

Thy pleasing smiles and grace,
          Thy face,
Haue rauisht so my sprights:
That life is growne to nought,
          Through thought,
Of Loue which me affrights.

For fancies flames of fire,
          Aspire,
Vnto such furious powre:
As but the teares I shead,
          Make dead,
The brands would me deuoure.

I should consume to nought,
          Through thought,
Of thy faire shining eie:
Thy cheekes, thy pleasing smiles,
          The wiles,
That forst my hart to die.

Thy grace, thy face, the part,
          Where art,
Stands gazing still to see:
The wondrous gifts and powre,
          Each howre,
That hath bewitched me.

                  T. L. Gent.

ALas my hart, mine eie hath wronged thee,
Presumptious eie, to gaze on Phillis face:
Whose heauenly eie, no mortall man may see,
But he must die, or purchase Phillis grace;
    Poore Coridon, the Nimph whose eie doth moue thee,
    Doth loue to draw, but is not drawne to loue thee.

Hir beautie, Natures pride, and Shepherds praise,
Hir eie, the heauenly Planet of my life,
Hir matchles wit, and grace, hir fame displaies,
As if that Ioue had made hir for his wife;
    Onely hir eies shoote firie darts to kill,
    Yet is hir hart, as cold as Caucase hill.

My wings too weake, to flie against the Sunne,
Mine eies vnable to sustaine hir light,
My hart doth yeeld, that I am quite vndoon,
Thus hath faire Phillis slaine me with hir sight:
    My bud is blasted, withered is my leafe,
    And all my corne is rotted in the sheafe.

Phillis, the golden fetter of my minde,
My fancies Idoll, and my vitall powre;
Goddesse of Nimphes, and honor of thy kinde,
This Ages Phenix, Beauties brauest bowre;
    Poore Coridon for loue of thee must die,
    Thy Beauties thrall, and conquest of thine eie.

Leaue Coridon, to plough the barren feeld,
Thy buds of hope are blasted with disgrace;
For Phillis lookes, no hartie loue doe yeeld,
Nor can she loue, for all hir louely face,
    Die Coridon, the spoyle of Phillis eie,
    She can not loue, and therefore thou must die.

WHat cunnnig can expresse   [read: *cunning*]
  The fauor of hir face,
To whom in this distresse,
I doe appeale for grace,
    A thousand Cupids flie,
    About hir gentle eie.

From whence each throwes a dart,
That kindleth soft sweete fier:
Within my sighing hart,
Possessed by desier:
    No sweeter life I trie,
    Than in hir loue to die.

The Lillie in the fielde,
That glories in his white:
For purenes now must yeelde,
And render vp his right:
    Heau'n pictur'de in hir face,
    Doth promise ioy and grace.

Faire Cinthias siluer light,
That beates on running streames;
Compares not with hir white,
Whose haires are all sunbeames;
    Hir vertues so doe shine,
    As daie vnto mine eine.

With this there is a Red,
Exceeds the Damaske Rose;
Which in hir cheekes is spred;
Whence euery fauor groes,
    In skie there is no starre,
    That she surmounts not farre.

When Phœbus from the bed,
Of Thetis doth arise,
The morning blushing red,
In faire carnation wise,

    He shewes it in hir face,
        As Queene of euery grace.

This pleasant Lillie white,
This taint of roseat red,
This Cinthias siluer light,
This sweete faire Dea spread,
    These sunbeames in mine eie,
    These beauties make me die.

E. O.

A most excellent passion set downe
by N. B. Gent.

COm yonglings com, that seem to make such mone,
About a thing of nothing God he knowes:
With sighes and sobs, and many a greeuous grone,
And trickling teares, that secret sorow showes,
    Leaue, leaue to faine, and here behold indeed,
    The onely man, may make your harts to bleed.

Whose state to tell; no, neuer toong can tell:
Whose woes are such; oh no, there are none such:
Whose hap so hard: nay rather halfe a hell:
Whose griefe so much: yea God he knowes too much:
    Whose wofull state, and greeuous hap (alas,)
    The world may see, is such as neuer was.

Good nature weepes to see hir selfe abused;
Ill fortune shewes hir furie in hir face:
Poore reason pines to see hir selfe refused:
And dutie dies, to see his sore disgrace.
    Hope hangs the head, to see dispaire so neere;
    And what but death can end this heauie cheere?

Oh cursed cares, that neuer can be knowne:
Dole, worse than death, when neuer tong can tell it:

The hurt is hid, although the sorow showne,
Such is my paine, no pleasure can expell it.
    In summe I see, I am ordained I:
    To liue in dole, and so in sorow die.
Behold each teare, no token of a toy:
But torments such, as teare my hart asunder:
Each sobbing sigh, a signe of such annoy,
That how I liue, beleeue me 'tis a wonder.
    Each grone, a gripe, that makes me gaspe for breath:
    And euerie straine, a bitter pang of death.

Loe thus I liue, but looking still to die:
And still I looke, but still I see in vaine:
And still in vaine, alas, I lie and crie:
And still I crie, but haue no ease of paine.
    So still in paine, I liue, looke, lie, and crie:
    When hope would helpe, or death would let me die.

Sometime I sleepe, a slumber, not a sleepe:
And then I dreame (God knowes) of no delight,
But of such woes, as makes me lie and weepe
Vntill I wake, in such a pitious plight;
    As who beheld me sleeping or awaking,
    Would say my hart were in a heauie taking.

Looke as the dew doth lie vpon the ground,
So sits the sweate of sorow on my face:
Oh deadly dart, that strooke so deepe a wound,
Oh hatefull hap, to hit in such a place:
    The hart is hurt, and bleedes the bodie ouer:
    Yet cannot die, nor euer health recouer.

Then he or she, that hath a happie hand,
To helpe a hart, that hath no hope to liue:
Come, come with speede, and do not staying stand:
But if no one, can any comfort giue,
    Run to the Church, and bid the Sexton toule
    A solemne knell, yet for a silie soule.

Harke how it sounds, that sorrow lasteth long:
Long, long: long long: long long, and longer yet:
Oh cruell death: thou doost me double wrong,
To let me lie so long in such a fit:
    Yet when I die, write neighbors where I lie;
    Long was I dead, ere death would let me die.

THese lines I send by waues of woe,
    And bale becomes my boate:
Which sighes of sorowes still shall keepe,
    On floods of feare afloate.

My sighes shall serue me still for winde,
    My lading is my smart:
And true report my pilot is,
    My hauen is thy hart.

My keele is fram'd of crabbed care,
    My ribs are all of ruthe:
My planks are nothing else but plants,
    With treenailes ioinde with truthe.

My maine mast made of nought but mone,
    My tackling trickling teares:
And Topyard like a troubled minde,
    A flagge of follie beares.

My Cable is a constant hart,
    My Anckor luckles Loue:
Which Reasons Capstones from the ground,
    Of griefe can not remoue.

My Decks are all of deepe disgrace,
    My Compas discontent;
And perill is my Northern Pole,
    And death my Orient.

My Saylers are my sorowing thoughts,
    The Boateswane bitter sence:
The Master, miserie; his mate
    Is dolefull diligence.

Sir W. H.

FEede still thy selfe, thou fondling with beliefe,
  Go hunt thy hope, that neuer tooke effect,
Accuse the wrongs that oft hath wrought thy griefe,
And reckon sure where reason would suspect.

Dwell in the dreames of wish and vaine desire,
Pursue the faith that flies and seekes to new,
Run after hopes that mocke thee with retire,
And looke for loue where liking neuer grew.

Deuise conceits to ease thy carefull hart,
Trust vpon times and daies of grace behinde,
Presume the rights of promise and desart,
And measure loue by thy beleeuing minde.

Force thy affects that spite doth daily chace,
Winke at the wrongs with wilfull ouersight,
See not the soyle and staine of thy disgrace,
Nor recke disdaine, to doate on thy delite.

And when thou seest the end of thy reward,
And these effects ensue of thine assault,
When rashnes rues, that reason should regard,
Yet still accuse thy fortune for the fault.
    And crie, O Loue, O death, O vaine desire,
      When thou complainst the heate, & feeds the fire.

MY first borne loue vnhappily conceiued,
Brought foorth in paine, & christened with a curse
Die in your Infancie, of life bereaued,
                        By your cruell nurse.

Restlesse desire, from my Loue that proceeded,
Leaue to be, and seeke your heauen by dieng,
Since you, O you? your owne hope haue exceeded,
                        By too hie flieng.

And you my words, my harts faithfull expounders,
No more offer your Iewell, vnesteemed,
Since those eies my Loues life and liues confounders,
                        Your woorth misdeemed.

Loue leaue to desire, words leaue it to vtter,
Swell on my thoughts, till you breake that contains you
My complaints in those deafe eares no more mutter,
                        That so disdaines you.

And you careles of me, that without feeling,
With drie eies, behold my Tragedie smiling,
Decke your proude triumphes with your poore slaues yeelding
                        To his owne spoyling.

But if that wrong, or holy truth dispised,
To iust reuenge, the heauens euer moued,
So let hir loue, and so be still denied,
                        Who she so loued.

THe brainsicke race that wanton youth ensues,
Without regard to grounded wisdomes lore,
As often as I thinke thereon, renues
The fresh remembrance of an ancient sore:
    Reuoking to my pensiue thoughts at last,
    The worlds of wickednes that I haue past.

And though experience bids me bite on bit,
And champe the bridle of a better smacke,
Yet costly is the price of after wit,
Which brings so cold repentance at hir backe:
    And skill that's with so many losses bought,
    Men say is little better worth than nought.

And yet this fruit I must confesse doth growe
Of follies scourge: that though I now complaine
Of error past, yet henceforth I may knowe
To shun the whip that threats the like againe:
    For wise men though they smart a while, had leuer
    To learne experience at the last, than neuer.

THose eies which set my fancie on a fire,
Those crisped haires, which hold my hart in chains,
Those daintie hands, which conquer'd my desire,
That wit, which of my thoughts doth hold the rains.

Those eies for cleernes doe the starrs surpas,
Those haires obscure the brightnes of the Sunne,
Those hands more white, than euer Iuorie was,
That wit euen to the skies hath glorie woon.

O eies that pearce our harts without remorse,
O haires of right that weares a roiall crowne,
O hands that conquer more than Cæsars force,
O wit that turns huge kingdoms vpside downe.

    Then Loue be Iudge, what hart may thee withstand:
    Such eies, such haire, such wit, and such a hand.

PRaisd be Dianas faire and harmles light,
Praisd be the dewes, wherwith she moists the ground;
Praisd be hir beames, the glorie of the night,
Praisd be hir powre, by which all powres abound.

Praisd be hir Nimphs, with whom she decks the woods,
Praisd be hir knights, in whom true honor liues,
Praisd be that force, by which she moues the floods,
Let that Diana shine, which all these giues.

In heauen Queene she is among the spheares,
In ay she Mistres like makes all things pure,
Eternitie in hir oft chaunge she beares,
She beautie is, by hir the faire endure.

Time weares hir not, she doth his chariot guide,
Mortalitie belowe hir orbe is plaste,
By hir the vertue of the starrs downe slide,
In hir is vertues perfect image cast.

   A knowledge pure it is hir worth to kno,
   With Circes let them dwell that thinke not so.

Like to a Hermite poore in place obscure,
I meane to spend my daies of endles doubt,
To waile such woes as time cannot recure,
Where none but Loue shall euer finde me out.

My foode shall be of care and sorow made,
My drink nought else but teares falne from mine eies,
And for my light in such obscured shade,
The flames shall serue, which from my hart arise.

A gowne of graie, my bodie shall attire,
My staffe of broken hope whereon Ile staie,
Of late repentance linckt with long desire,
The couch is fram'de whereon my limbes Ile lay,

   And at my gate dispaire shall linger still,
   To let in death when Loue and Fortune will.

Like truthles dreames, so are my ioyes expired,
And past returne, are all my dandled daies:
My loue misled, and fancie quite retired,
Of all which past, the sorow onely staies.

My lost delights, now cleane from sight of land,
Haue left me all alone in vnknowne waies:
My minde to woe, my life in fortunes hand,
Of all which past, the sorow onely staies.

As in a countrey strange without companion,
I onely waile the wrong of deaths delaies,
Whose sweete spring spent, whose sommer wel nie don,
Of all which past, the sorow onely staies.

  Whom care forewarnes, ere age and winter colde,
  To haste me hence, to finde my fortunes folde.

A Secret murder hath bene done of late,
Vnkindnes founde, to be the bloudie knife,
And shee that did the deede a dame of state,
Faire, gracious, wise, as any beareth life.

To quite hir selfe, this answere did she make,
Mistrust (quoth she) hath brought him to his end,
Which makes the man so much himselfe mistake,
To lay the guilt vnto his guiltles frend.

Ladie not so, not feard I found my death,
For no desart thus murdered is my minde,
And yet before I yeeld my fainting breath,
I quite the killer, tho I blame the kinde.

  You kill vnkinde, I die, and yet am true,
  For at your sight, my wound doth bleede anew.

Sought by the world, and hath the world disdain'd,
Is she, my hart, for whom thou doost endure,
Vnto whose grace, sith Kings haue not obtaind,
Sweete is thy choise, though losse of life be sowre:
    Yet to the man, whose youth such pains must proue,
    No better end, than that which comes by Loue.

Steere then thy course vnto the port of death,
Sith thy hard hap no better hap may finde,
Where when thou shalt vnlade thy latest breath,
Enuie hir selfe shall swim to saue thy minde,
    Whose bodie sunke in search to gaine that shore,
    Where many a Prince had perished before.

And yet my hart it might haue been foreseene,
Sith skilfull medcins mends each kinde of griefe,
Then in my breast full safely hadst thou beene,
But thou my hart wouldst neuer me beleeue,
    Who tolde thee true, when first thou didst aspire,
    Death was the end of euery such desire.

Hir face,   Hir tong,   Hir wit,
So faire,   So sweete,   So sharpe,
First bent,   Then drew,   Then hit,
Mine eie,   Mine eare,   My hart.

Mine eie,   Mine eare,   My hart,
To like,   To learne,   To loue,
Hir face,   Hir tong,   Hir wit,
Doth lead,   doth teach,   Doth moue.

Oh face,   Oh tong,   Oh wit,
With frownes,   With checke,   With smart,
Wrong not,   Vexe not,   Wound not,
Mine eie,   Mine eare,   My hart.

Mine eie,   Mine eare,   My hart,
To learne,   To knowe,   To feare,

| Hir face, | Hir tong, | Hir wit, |
| Doth lead, | Doth teach, | Doth sweare. |

Calling to minde mine eie long went about,
T'entice my hart to seeke to leaue my brest,
All in a rage I thought to pull it out,
By whose deuice I liu'd in such vnrest,
    What could it say to purchase so my grace?
    Forsooth that it had seene my Mistres face.

Another time I likewise call to minde,
My hart was he that all my woe had wrought,
For he my brest the fort of Loue resignde,
When of such warrs my fancie neuer thought,
    What could it say, when I would him haue slaine?
    But he was yours, and had forgone me cleane.

At length when I perceiu'd both eie and hart,
Excusde themselues, as guiltles of mine ill,
I found my selfe was cause of all my smart,
And tolde my selfe, my selfe now slay I will:
    But when I found my selfe to you was true,
    I lou'd my selfe, bicause my selfe lou'd you.

WHat else is hell, but losse of blisfull heauen?
    What darknes else, but lacke of lightsome day?
What else is death, but things of life bereauen?
What winter else, but pleasant springs decay?

Vnrest what else, but fancies hot desire,
Fed with delay, and followed with dispaire?
What else mishap, but longing to aspire,
To striue against, earth, water, fire and aire?

Heauen were my state, and happie Sunneshine day,
And life most blest, to ioy one howres desire,

Hap, blisse, and rest, and sweete springtime of May,
Were to behold my faire consuming fire.

But loe, I feele, by absence from your sight,
Mishap, vnrest, death, winter, hell, darke night.

WOuld I were chaung'd into that golden showre,
   That so diuinely streamed from the skies,
To fall in drops vpon the daintie floore,
Where in hir bed, she solitarie lies,
    Then would I hope such showres as richly shine,
    Would pearce more deepe than these wast teares of mine.

Or would I were that plumed Swan, snowe white,
Vnder whose forme, was hidden heauenly power,
Then in that riuer would I most delite,
Whose waues doe beate, against hir stately bower,
    And in those banks, so tune my dying song,
    That hir deafe ears, would think my plaint too long.

Else would I were, Narcissus, that sweete boy,
And she hir selfe, the sacred fountaine cleere,
Who rauisht with the pride of his owne ioy,
Drenched his lims, with gazing ouer neere:
    So should I bring, my soule to happie rest,
    To end my life, in that I loued best.

WHo plucks thee down from hie desire poor hart? Care.
   Who comforts thee in depth of thy distresse? Care.
Amid contents, who breeds thy secret smart? Care.
Who seekes the meane, thy sorrowes may be lesse? Care.

Who calls thy wits togither to their worke: Care.
Who warnes thy will, to follow warie wit? Care.
Who lets thee see in loue what sorrowes lurke? Care.
Who makes thee feele the force of fancies fit? Care.

Who taught thee first to trie before thou trust?	Care.
Who bids thee keepe a faithfull tried freend?	Care.
Who wils thee say, loue wantons he that lust?	Care.
Who winnes the wish, that hath a happie end?	Care.

    Care then to keepe, that faithfull friend in store,
    Whose loue commands, that thou shalt care no more.

THose eies that holds the hand of euery hart,
Those hands that holds the hart of euery eie,
That wit that goes beyond all natures Art,
That sence too deepe, for wisdome to discrie,
    That eie, that hand, that wit, that heauenly sence,
    All these doth show my Mistres Excellence.

Oh eies that perce into the purest hart,
Oh hands that hold, the highest harts in thrall,
Oh wit that weyes the deapth of all desart,
Oh sence that showes, the secret sweete of all,
    The heauen of heuens, with heuenly powrs preserue thee,
    Loue but thy selfe, and giue me leaue to serue thee.

To serue, to liue, to looke vpon those eies,
To looke, to liue, to kisse that heauenlie hand,
To sound that wit, that doth amaze the wise,
To know that sence, no sence can vnderstand,
    To vnderstande that all the world may know,
    Such wit, such sence, eies, hands, there are no moe.

WHo list to heare the sum of sorrowes state,
The depth of dole, wherein a minde may dwell,
The loathed life, that happie harts may hate,
The saddest tale, that euer toong could tell,
    But reade this verse, and say who wrote the same,
    Doth onely dwell, where comfort neuer came.

A carefull head, first crost with crooked hap,
A wofull wit, bewitcht with wretched will,
A clyming hart, falne downe from Fortunes lap,
A bodie borne, to loose his labour still,
    A mourning minde, sore mated with despite,
    May serue to shewe, the lacke of my delite.

Yet more than this, a hope still founde in vaine,
A vile dispaire, that speakes but of distresse,
A forst content, to suffer deadly paine,
A paine so great, as can not get redresse,
    Will all affirme, my sum of sorrow such,
    As neuer man, that euer knew so much.

AS rare to heare, as seldome to be seene,
It can not be, nor euer yet hath beene,
That fire should burne, with perfect heate and flame,
Without some matter for to yeeld the same.

A straunger case, yet true by proofe I knowe,
A man in ioye, that liued still in woe,
Burnt with desire, and doth posses at will,
Enioying all, yet all desiring still.

Who hath ynough, yet thinks he liues without,
To want no loue, and yet to stand in doubt,
What discontent, to liue in such desire,
To haue his will, yet euer to require.

THe time, when first I fell in Loue,
    Which now I must lament,
The yeere, wherein I lost such time,
    to compasse my content.

The day, wherein I sawe too late,
    The follies of a Louer,

The hower, wherein I found such losse,
    As care cannot recouer.

And last, the minute of mishap,
    Which makes me thus to plaine,
The dolefull fruits of Louers sutes,
    Which labor lose in vaine:

Doth make me solemnly protest,
    As I with paine doe proue,
There is no time, yeere, day, nor howre,
    Nor minute, good to loue.

WHen day is gone, and darknes come,
    The toyling tired wight,
Doth vse to ease his wearie bones,
    By rest in quiet night.

When storme is staied, and harbor woon,
    The Sea man set on shore,
With comfort doth requite the care,
    Of perils past before.

When loue hath woon, where it did woo,
    And light where it delites,
Contented minde, thenceforth forgets,
    The frowne of former spites.

THough neither tears nor torments can be thought,
    Nor death it selfe too deere to be sustaind,
To win those ioyes so woorthie to be sought,
So rare to reach, so sweete to be obtaind.

Yet earnest Loue, with longing to aspire,
To that which hope holds in so high regarde,

Makes time delaid, a torment to desire,
When Loue with hope forbeares his iust rewarde.

   Then blessed hope haste on thy happie daies,
   Saue my desire, by shortning thy delaies.

A notable description of the World.

OF thick and thin, light, heauie, dark and cleere,	Mixtures.
White, black, & blew, red, green, & purple die:	Coulors.
Gold, Siluer, Brasse, Lead, Iron, Tin, and Copper,	Mettals.
Moist aire, hot fire, cold water, earth full drie:	Elements.
Blood, Choler, Flegme, and Melancholie by,	Complexions
A mixed masse, a Chaos all confusde,	Chaos.
Such was the world, till God diuision vsde.	

In framing heau'n and earth, God did diuide,	
The first daies light, and darkth, to night and day.	1
The second, he a firmament applide,	2
Third, fruitfull earth appeerd, Seas tooke their way,	3
Fourth, Sun and Moone, with Stars in skies he fixt,	4
Fift, Fish and Foule, the Sea and land possest,	5
And God made Man, like to himselfe, the sixt:	6
The seauenth day, when all things he had blest:	7
He hallowed that, and therein tooke his rest.	

              W. S. Gent.

BY wracke late driuen on shoare, from Cupids Crare,
Whose sailes of error, sighes of hope and feare,
Conueied through seas of teares, and sands of care,
Till rocks of high disdaine, hir sides did teare,
   I write a dirge, for dolefull doues to sing,
   With selfe same quill, I pluckt from Cupids wing.

Farewell vnkinde, by whom I fare so ill,
Whose looks bewitcht my thoughts with false surmise,
Till forced reason did vnbinde my will,
And shewed my hart, the follie of mine eies,
    And saide, attending where I should attaine,
    Twixt wish and want, was but a pleasing paine.

Farewell vnkinde, my floate is at an ebbe,
My troubled thoughts, are turnd to quiet wars,
My fancies hope hath spun and spent hir webbe,
My former wounds, are closed vp with skars,
    As ashes lie, longe since consumde with fire,
    So is my loue, so now is my desire.

Farewell vnkinde, my first and finall loue,
Whose coie contempts, it bootes not heere to name,
But gods are iust, and euery star aboue,
Doth threat reuenge, where faith's reward is blame,
    And I may liue, though your despised thrall,
    By fond mischoyce, to see your fortunes fall.

Farewell vnkinde, most cruell of your kinde,
By whom my worth, is drowned in disdaines,
As was my loue, so is your iudgement blinde,
My fortune ill, and such hath bene my gaines,
    But this for all, I list no more to saie,
    Farewell faire proude, not lifes, but loues decaie.

THe gentle season of the yeere,
Hath made my blooming branch appeere,
    And beautified the land with flowres,
The aire doth sauor with delight,
The heauens doe smile, to see the sight,
    And yet mine eies, augments their showres.

The meades are mantled all with greene,
The trembling leaues, haue cloth'd the treene,
    The birds with feathers new doe sing,

But I poore soule, when wrong doth wrack,
Attyres my selfe in mourning black,
    Whose leafe doth fall amid his spring.

And as you see the skarlet Rose,
In his sweete prime, his buds disclose,
    Whose hewe is with the Sun reuiued,
So in the Aprill of mine age,
My liuely colours doe asswage,
    Because my Sun-shine is depriued.

My hart that wonted was of yore,
Light as the winde abroad to sore,
    Amongst the buds when beautie springs,
Now onely houers ouer you,
As doth the birde thats taken new,
    And mourns when all hir neighbours sings.

When euery man is bent to sport,
Then pensiue I alone resort,
    Into some solitarie walke,
As doth the dolefull Turtle doue,
Who hauing lost hir faithfull loue,
    Sits mourning on fome withered stalke.

There to my selfe, I doe recount,
How far my woes, my ioyes surmount,
    How Loue requiteth me with hate:
How all my pleasures end in paine,
How hate doth say, my hope is vaine,
    How fortune frownes vpon my state.

And in this moode, charg'd with despaire,
With vapored sighes, I dim the aire,
    And to the Gods make this request:
That by the ending of my life,
I may haue truce with this strange strife,
    And bring my soule to better rest.

A Counterloue.

DEclare O minde, from fond desires excluded,
That thou didst find erewhile, by Loue deluded.

An eie, the plot, whereon Loue sets his gin,
Beautie, the trap, wherein the heedles fall,
A smile, the traine, that drawes the simple in,
Sweete words, the wilie instrument of all,
    Intreaties posts, faire promises are charmes,
    Writing, the messenger, that wooes our harmes.

Mistresse, and seruant, titles of mischaunce:
Commaundments done, the act of slauerie,
Their coulors worne, a clownish cognisaunce,
And double dutie, pettie drudgerie,
    And when she twines and dallies with thy locks,
    Thy freedome then is brought into the stocks.

To touch hir hand, hir hand bindes thy desire,
To weare hir ring, hir ring is Nessus gift,
To feele hir brest, hir brest doth blowe the fire,
To see hir bare, hir bare a balefull drift,
    To baite thine eies thereon, is losse of sight,
    To thinke of it, confounds thy senses quite.

Kisses the keies, to sweete consuming sin,
Closings, Cleopatras adders at thy brest,
Fained resistance then she will begin,
And yet vnsatiable in all the rest,
    And when thou doost vnto the act proceede,
    The bed doth grone, and tremble at the deede.

Beautie, a siluer dew that falls in May,
Loue is an Egshell, with that humor fild,
Desire, a winged boy, comming that way,
Delights and dallies with it in the field,
    The firie Sun, drawes vp the shell on hie,
    Beautie decaies, Loue dies, desire doth flie.

Vnharmd giue eare, that thing is hap'ly caught,
That cost some deere, if thou maist ha't for naught.

AS ioy of ioyes, and neuer dying blis,
Is to behold that mightie powre diuine,
Nor may we craue more blessednes than this,
With face to face, to see his glorie shine,
   So heere on earth, the onely good I finde
   Is your sweete sight, my whole content of minde.

If to the hart, mine eie doth truthe impart,
More faire of late, than erst before you seeme,
Which beautie, though it breede my endles smart,
Yet still I loue and worthily esteeme,
   And if those beames, would shine vpon me still,
   Then had I heauen, and happines at will.

Some things by smelling liue, as fame report,
And some the water ioy, to their desire,
The subtile ayre, contents another sort,
And other some by taste and touch of fire,
   If such can liue with things of small delight,
   Much more should I, enioying of your sight.

SEt me where Phœbus heate, the flowers slaieth,
Or where continuall snowe withstands his forces,
Set me where he his temprate raies displaieth,
Or where he comes, or where he neuer courses.

Set me in Fortunes grace, or else discharged,
In sweete and pleasant aire, or darke and glooming,
Where daies and nights, are lesser, or inlarged,
In yeeres of strength, in failing age, or blooming.

Set me in heauen, or earth, or in the center,
Lowe in a vale, or on a mountaine placed,

Set me to daunger, perill, and aduenture,
Graced by Fame, or infamie disgraced.

   Set me to these, or anie other triall,
   Except my Mistres anger and deniall.

I Sawe the eies, that haue my seeing bounde,
  I harde the toong, that made my speech to staie,
Hir wit, my thoughts did captiue and confounde,
And with hir graces, drew my life away,
   Vnto hir life, in whom my sences liues,
   My spirit vp himselfe, for tribute giues.

She sawe mine eies, and they recouer'd light,
She spake to me, and I had powre to speake,
She graced me, and I regained spright,
She freed my hart, that readie was to breake,
   My life, that erst beginning had in me,
   Now by hir being, doth begin to be.

Mine eies, behold the beautie raignes in hir,
Speake toong of hir, that nothing is but wonder,
To honor hir, my spirits onely stir,
Serue hir my hart, or hart deuide asunder:
   And life, liue in the fauor she hath showne,
   Whereby thou hast more strength than was thine owne.

   Mistres, this grace, vnto your seruant giue,
   Thus for to liue, or not at all to liue.

N Arcissus neuer by desire distressed,
  Elected for the solace of his dwelling,
The diuers coullerd Medowe liuely dressed,
And fed with currant fresh, of waters swelling.

The while he liues in libertie, thrise blessed,
Loue sees, and enuieth his life excelling,
And in the waters streight, a shape expressed,
The poyson of his life, and freedomes quelling.

So carelesse I, that romed foorth vnarmed,
Not dreading Loue, who watches rebels narrow,
No sooner sawe hir eies, than inlie warmed,
With vnperceiued flames within the marrow.

And yet of both, my selfe most deepely harmed,
With waters he? I with a burning arrow,
He drown'd in waues, the which his teares did cherish,
I liue in fire, and die; and yet not perish.

THe firmament, with golden stars adorned,
The Saylers watchfull eies, full well contenteth,
And afterward with tempest ouerspred,
The absent lights of heauen, he sore lamenteth.

Your face, the firmament of my repose,
Long time haue kept, my waking thoughts delighted,
But now the clouds of sorrow ouergoes
Your glorious skies, wherewith I am affrighted.

For I that haue my life and fortunes placed,
Within the ship, that by those planets saileth,
By enuious chaunce, am ouermuch disgraced,
Seeing the Loadstar of my courses faileth.

 And yet content to drowne, without repining,
  To haue my stars affoord the world their shining.

CEase restles thoughts, surcharg'd with heauines,
Loue, fortune, and disdaine, with their endeuer,

The forces of my life will soone disseuer,
Without the sting of your vnquietnes.

And thou oh hart, guiltie of my distresse,
To harbor these faire foes, doost still perseuer,
Whereby thou shewst false traitor, thou hadst leuer
Their conquest, than mine ease and happines.

In thee, Loues messengers haue taken dwelling,
Fortune in thee, hir pompe triumphant spreadeth,
Disdaine hath spent on thee, hir bitter swelling,
Thus thou the root, from whence my woes proceedeth.

    Cease then vain thoughts, no more my sorows double.
    Loue, fortune, and disdaine, ynough of trouble.

THinking vpon the name, by Loue engraued,
    Within my hart, to be my liues directer,
The value of the whole entirely saued,
I reade vpon the sillables this lecter,
    Maruell, the first into my spirits soundeth,
    And maruelling at hir, the maruell woundeth.

I seeke to Gaine, as by the second's ment,
An interest in this admired maruaile,
But cannot finde a meane sufficient,
So hie a rated Gem to counteruaile,
    There is no weight in fire ordaind to shine,
    Nor counterworth of any thing diuine.

The last doth giue me counsell to Retire,
And rest content, that Loue hath blest my sight,
And toucht my fancie with th'immortall fire,
Of this diuine, and precious Margaret,
    And thanke my fortune of exceeding fauour,
    As to be thralled to so sweete behauiour.

O See my hart, vncertaine what effect,
   Shall finally ensue so high a scope,
See what it is, a Master to neglect,
To haue a Mistres entertaind on hope,
   He whom it was thy fortune first to serue,
   As she doth now, could neuer see thee sterue.

There meanly lodg'd, yet mery were thy daies,
Here, high conceited intermixt with feare,
There, words and works all one, here great delaies,
There, things were in their kinde, here as they were,
   Thy hopes there small, but yet assured Loue,
   And here though great, God knowes if any proue.

Yet must I not discourage thine intent,
All paines and torments suffred for hir sake,
May be in fine well answerd by euent,
If so thy sute in time effect may take,
   But tell hir what thy former Master saies,
   Cursed is he that dieth through delaies.

TO make a truce, sweete Mistres with your eies,
   How often haue I proffred you my hart,
Which profers vnesteemed you despise,
As far to meane, to equall your desart,
   Your minde wherein, all hie perfections flowe,
   Deignes not the thought, of things that are so lowe.

To striue to alter his desires, were vaine,
Whose vowed hart, affects no other place,
The which since you despise, I doe disdaine,
To count it mine, as erst before it was:
   For that is mine, which you alone alow,
   As I am yours, and onely liue for you.

Now if I him forsake, and he not finde,
His wretched exile, succord by your eies,
He can not yeeld, to serue anothers minde,

Nor liue alone, for nature that denies,
    Then die he must, for other choise is none,
    But liue in you, or me, or die alone.

Whose haples death, when Fame abroad hath blowne,
Blame and reproch, procures vnto vs both,
I, as vnkinde, forsaking so mine owne,
But you much more, from whom the rigour groweth,
    And so much more, will your dishonor be,
    By how much more, it loued you than me.

    Sweete Ladie then, the harts misfortune rue,
    Whose loue and seruice euermore was true.

SEeing those eies, that with the Sun contendeth,
For maiestie of light, and excellence,
A quickning pleasure secretly descendeth
Into my hart, by subtill influence.

Not seeing them, horror my blisse depriueth,
And I, as one, by publike lawe conuicted,
Whom rigorouslie, the hedsman onward driueth
To shamefull death, most heauily afflicted.

I onely liue, when I behold your shining,
Bright stars, rare lights, sweete authors of my gladnes,
Absent from you, my hart in sorrow pining,
Doth feede on teares, on anguish, griefe, and sadnes.

    Then maruell not, if I desire accesse,
    Vnto the fountaine of my happines.

TO shun the death, my rare and chosen Iuell,
    That couertly, within your eies soiourneth,
I flie, and flying feele the fire, more cruell,
Wherewith offended, loue my spirits burneth.

A death most painfull, and the paine more bitter,
Then I returne, resolued in opinion,
Since I must die, neere, or farre of, tys fitter,
To end my life, within hir eies dominion.

O then displaie (faire Eies) your influence,
That I, into the deeper flames ascending,
Fall soone to ashes, by hir excellence,
And better be contented with my ending.

    And all remooued, that my quiet hinders,
    Rake vp both loue, and life, within those cinders.

OF all the woes my pensiue hart endureth,
It greeues me most, when I my sorrowes frame,
I knowe not what, this wretchednes procureth,
Nor whereupon I am to cast the blame.

The fault is not in hir, for well I see,
I am vnworthy of hir grace, in this,
Nor yet in loue, who hath vouchsafed me,
To knowe within this life so rare a blisse.

To grieue me of my sight, then comes to minde,
As head and author of my haples woes:
But better afterward aduisde, I finde,
That onely from hir lookes, all sweetnes floes.

    And when iust cause of sorrowing doth faile,
    I waile in fine, bicause I cannot waile.

DIuide my times, and rate my wretched howres,
From day to month, from month to many yeeres,
And then compare my sweetest to my sowres,
To see which more in equall view appeeres,

    And iudge, if for my daies and yeeres of care,
    I haue but howres of comfort to compare.

Iust and not much, it were in these extreemes,
So hard a touch, and torment of the thought,
For any minde, that any right esteemes,
To yeeld so small delite, so deerely bought,
    But he that liues but in his owne despite,
    Is not to finde his fortune by his right.

The life that still runs forth hir wearie waies,
With sowre to sawce the dainties of delite,
And care to choake the pleasure of hir daies,
And no rewarde, those many wrongs to quite,
    No blame to holde such irksome time in hate,
    As but to losse, prolongs a wretched state.

And so I loath, euen to behold the light,
That shines without all pleasure to mine eies,
With greedie wish, I wait still for the night,
Yet neither this I finde, that may suffice,
    Not that I holde, the day in more delight,
    But that alike, I loath both day and night.

The day I see, yeelds but increase to care,
The night that should, by nature serue to rest,
Against hir kinde, denies such ease to spare,
As pitie would affoord the soule opprest,
    And broken sleepes oft times present in sight,
    A dreaming wish, beguild with false delight.

The sleepe, or else what so for sweete appeeres,
Is vnto me but pleasure in despite,
The flowre of age, the name of yonger yeeres,
Doe but vsurpe the title of delite,
    For carefull thought, and sorow sundry waies,
    Consumes my youth, before my aged daies.

The touch, the sting, the torment of desire,
To striue beyond the compas of restraint,

Kept from the reach whereto it would aspire,
Giues cause (God knowes) too iust to my complaint,
   Besides the wrongs, which now with my distresse,
   My meaning is, in silence to suppresse.

Oft with my selfe, I enter in deuice,
To reconcile these wearie thoughts to peace,
I treat for truce, I flatter and entice,
My wrangling wits, to worke for their release,
   But all in vaine, I seeke the meanes to finde,
   That might appease, the discord of my minde.

For when I force a fained mirth in shoe,
And would forget, and so beguile my greefe,
I cannot rid my selfe of sorow so,
Altho I feede vpon a false beleefe,
   For inward touch of vncontented minde,
   Returns my cares, by course vnto their kinde.

Wainde from my will, and thus by triall taught,
How for to holde, all fortune in regard,
Though heere I boast, a knowledge deerely bought,
Yet this poore gaine, I reape for my reward,
   I learne hereby, to harden and prepare,
   A readie minde, for all assaults of care.

Whereto, as one, euen from my cradle borne,
And not to looke for better to ensue,
I yeeld my selfe, and wish these times outworne,
That but remaine, my torments to renue,
   And leaue to those, these daies of my despite,
   Whose better hap, may liue to more delite.

A description of Loue.

Now what is Loue, I praie thee tell,
It is that fountaine and that well,
Where pleasure and repentance dwell,

It is perhaps that sauncing bell,
    That tols all in to heauen or hell,
    And this is Loue as I heare tell.

Yet what is Loue, I praie thee saie?
It is a worke, on holie daie,
It is December matcht with Maie,
When lustie blouds in fresh araie,
    Heare ten months after of the plaie,
    And this is Loue as I heare saie.

Yet what is Loue, I praie thee saine?
It is a Sunshine mixt with raine,
It is a tooth ache, or like paine,
It is a game, where none doth gaine,
    The Lasse saith no, and would full faine,
    And this is Loue, as I heare saine.

Yet what is Loue, I pray thee say,
It is a yea, it is a nay,
A pretie kinde of sporting fray,
It is a thing will soone away:
    Then take the vantage while you may,
    And this is Loue, as I heare say.

Yet what is Loue I pray thee shoe,
A thing that creepes, it cannot goe,
A prize that passeth to and fro,
A thing for one, a thing for mo,
    And he that proues must finde it so,
    And this is Loue (sweet friend) I troe.

The description of Iealousie.

A Seeing friend, yet enimie to rest,   [read: *seeming*]
  A wrangling passion, yet a gladsom thought,
A bad companion, yet a welcom guest,

A knowledge wisht, yet found too soone vnsought,
    From heauen supposde, yet sure condemn'd to hell,
    Is Iealousie, and there forlorne doth dwell.

And thence doth send fond feare and false suspect,
To haunt our thoughts bewitched with mistrust,
Which breedes in vs the issue and effect,
Both of conceits and actions far vniust,
    The griefe, the shame, the smart, wherof doth proue,
    That Iealousie's both death and hell to Loue.

For what but hell moues in the iealous hart,
Where restles feare works out all wanton ioyes,
Which doth both quench and kill the louing part,
And cloies the minde with worse than knowne annoyes,
    Whose pressure far exceeds hells deepe extreemes,
    Such life leads Loue entangled with misdeemes.

AH poore Conceit, delite is dead,
    Thy pleasant daies are doon,
The shadie dales must be his walke,
    That cannot see the sunne.

The world I now to witnes call,
    The heauens my records be:
If euer I were false to Loue,
    Or Loue were true to me.

I knowe it now, I knew it not,
    But all too late I rew it,
I rew not that I knew it not,
    But that I euer knew it.

My care is not a fond conceit,
    That breedes a fained smart,
My griefes doe gripe me at the gall,
    And gnaw me at the hart.

My teares are not those fained drops,
    That fall from fancies eies,
But bitter streams of strange distresse,
    Wherein discomfort lies.

My sighes are not those heauie sighes,
    That showes a sickly breath,
My passions are the perfect signes,
    And very paines of death.

In sum to make a dolefull end,
    To see my death so nie,
That sorow bids me sing my last,
    And so my senses die.

SHort is my rest, whose toile is ouerlong,
My ioyes are darke, but cleere I see my woe,
My safetie small: great wracks I bide by wrong,
Whose time is swift, and yet my hap but sloe,
    Each griefe and wound, in my poore hart appeeres,
    That laugheth howres, and weepeth many yeeres.

Deedes of the day, are fables for the night,
Sighes of desire, are smoakes of thoughtfull teares,
My steps are false, although my paths be right,
Disgrace is bolde, and fauor full of feares,
    Disquiet sleepe, keepes audit of my life,
    Where rare content, doth make displeasure rife.

The dolefull bell, that is the voice of time,
Cals on my end, before my haps be seene,
Thus fals my hopes, whose harmes haue power to clime,
Not come to haue that long in wish hath beene,
    I seeke your loue, and feare not others hate,
    Be you with me, and I haue Cæsars state.

The praise of Virginitie.

Virginitie resembleth right the Rose,
    That gallantly within the garden growes,
    Whilst in the mothers bodie it doth stand,
Of nibling sheep vntoucht, or shepherds hand.
The aire thereon, and ruddie morne doth smile,
The earth and waters, fauours it that while,
Braue lustie youth, and the inamord Dame,
Euen so doth age, and temples craue the same.

But when from naturall stalke, it is remou'd,
And place where it, so highly was belou'd,
The grace that earth, and heauen thereon did cast,
With beautie, fauor, loue, and all, is past.
Euen so the Maid, when once hir flowre is lost,
More deere than eie, or life, or what is most,
The loue and liking which she had before,
Forgoeth quite, and she esteem'd no more.

    Ladies Lenuoy to you that haue this prize,
    I reed ye hold your owne, if you be wise.

O Night, O ielious night, repugnant to my pleasures,
    O night so long desir'd, yet crosse to my content,
Ther's none but onely thou that can performe my pleasures,
Yet none but onely thou that hindereth my intent.

Thy beams, thy spiteful beams, thy lamps that burn to brightly,
Discouer all my traines, and naked lay my drifts,
That night by night I hope, yet faile my purpose nightly,
Thy enuious glaring gleame defeateth so my shifts.

Sweet night withhold thy beams, withhold them til to morow,
Whose ioyes in lack so long, a hell of torments breedes,
Sweete night, sweete gentle night, doe not prolong my sorow,
Desire is guide to me, and Loue no Loadstar needes.

Let Sailers gaze on stars and Moone so freshly shining,
Let them that misse the way be guided by the light,
I knowe my Ladies bowre, there needes no more diuining,
Affection sees in darke, and Loue hath eies by night.

Dame Cinthia couch awhile, holde in thy hornes for shining,
And glad not lowring night, with thy too glorious raies,
But be she dim and darke, tempestuous and repining,
That in hir spite, my sport may worke thy endles praise.

And when my will is wrought, then Cinthia shine good Ladie,
All other nights and daies, in honour of that night,
That happie heauenly night, that night so darke and shadie,
Wherein my Loue had eies, that lighted my delight.

SWeete Violets (Loues paradice) that spred
    Your gracious odours, which you couched beare,
        Within your palie faces,
Vpon the gentle wing of some calme breathing winde,
   That plaies amidst the plaine,
    If by the fauour of propicious stars you gaine,
Such grace as in my Ladies bosome place to finde,
     Be prowd to touch those places,
   And when hir warmth your moisture forth doth wear,
Whereby hir daintie parts are sweetly fed,
    Your honors of the flowrie meads I pray,
    You pretie daughters of the earth and Sun,
     With milde and seemly breathing straight display,
    My bitter sighes that haue my hart vndoon.

Vermilion Roses that with new daies rise,
   Display your Crimsen folds fresh looking faire,
     Whose radiant bright, disgraces
The rich adorned raies of Roseat rising morne,
   (Ah) if hir virgins hand
    Doe pluck your pure, ere Phœbus view the land,
And vaile your gracious pomp in louely natures scorne,

    If chaunce my Mistres traces,
  Fast by your flowres to take the Sommers aire,
Then wofull blushing tempt hir glorious eies,
    To spread their teares Adonis death reporting,
    And tell Loues torments sorowing for hir frend,
    Whose drops of blood within your leaus consorting
    Report faire Venus mones withouten end.

  Then may remorse (in pitying of my smart)
  Drie vp my teares, and dwell within hir hart.

Avrora now, began to rise againe,
From watrie couch, and from old Tithons side,
In hope to kisse vpon Acteian plaine,
Yong Cephalus, and through the golden glide,

On Easterne coast, she cast so great a light,
That Phœbus thought it time to make retire,
From Thetis Bowre, wherein he spent the night,
To light the world againe with heauenly fire.

Nor sooner gan his winged steedes to chase,
The Stigian night, mantled with duskie vale,
But poore Amyntas, hasteth him apace,
In desarts thus, to weepe a wofull tale.

Now silent shades, and all that dwell therein,
As Birds, or Beasts, or Wormes that creepe on grounde,
Dispose your selues to teares, while I begin,
To rew the griefe, of mine eternall wounde.

And dolefull ghosts, whose nature flies the light,
Come seate your selues with me on eu'ry side,
And whilst I die for want of my delight,
Lament the woes that Fancie me betide.

Phillis is dead, the marke of my desire,
My cause of loue, and shipwracke of my ioyes,

Phillis is gone, that set my hart on fire,
That clad my thoughts with ruinous annoyes.

Phillis is fled, and bides I wot not where,
Phillis (alas) the praise of woman kinde,
Phillis the Sun of this our hemisphere,
Whose beames made me and many others blinde.

But blinded me (poore man) aboue the rest,
That like olde Oedipus, I liue in thrall,
Still feele the worst, and neuer hope the best,
My mirth in mone, my honie drownd in gall.

Hir faire, but cruell eies, bewitcht my sight,
Hir sweete, but fading speech, enthrald my thought,
And in hir deeds, I reaped such delight,
As brought both will, and libertie to nought.

Therefore all hope of happines adue,
Adue desire the source of all my care,
Dispaire me tels my weale will nere renue,
Till this my soule, doth passe in Charons Crare.

Meane time my minde must suffer Fortunes skorne,
My thoughts stil wound, like wounds that stil are green
My weakned lyms, be laide on beds of thorne,
My life decaies, although my death foreseene.

Mine eies, now eies no more, but seas of teares,
Weepe on your fill, to coole my burning brest,
Where Loue did place desire, twixt hope, and feares,
(I saie) desire, the author of vnrest.

And (would to gods) Phillis where ere thou be,
Thy soule did see, the sowre of mine estate,
My ioyes eclipst, for onely want of thee,
My being with my selfe at foule debate.

My humble vowes, my sufferance of woe,
My sobs, and sighes, my euerwatching eies,

My plaintife teares, my wandring to and froe,
My will to die, my neuer ceasing cries.

No doubt but then, thy sorrows would perswade,
The doome of death, to cut my vitall twist,
That I with thee, amidst th'infernall shade,
And thou with me, might sport vs as we list.

O if thou waite on faire Proserpines traine,
And hearest Orpheus, neere th'Elisian springs,
Entreat thy Queene, to free thee thence againe,
And let the Thracian guide thee with his strings.

T. W. Gent.

AWay dispaire, the death of hopeles harts,
For hope and truth, assure me long agoe,
That pleasure is the end of lingring smarts,
When time, with iust content, rewardeth woe.

Sweete vertues throne is built in labours towre,
Where Lawrell wreath's are twist for them alone,
Whose gals are burst with often taste of sowre,
Whose blis from bale is sprong, whose mirth from mone.

I therefore striue by toyles, to raise my name,
And Iason like, to gaine a golden fleece,
The end of eu'ry worke doth crowne the same,
As witnes well, the happie harmes of Greece:

    For if the Greekes, had soone got Pryams seat,
    The glory of their paines, had not been great.

T. W. Gent.

I Hope and feare, that for my weale or woe,
That heau'nly lampe, which yeelds both heat & light,
To make a throne, for gods on earth belowe,
Is cut in twaine, and fixt in my delight,
    Which two faire hemyspheres, through light & heat,
    Planting desire, driue reason from hir seate.

No, no, my too forgetfull toong blaspheames,
I should haue saide, that where these hemispheres,
In harts, through eies, fixe hot and lightsome beames,
There reason works desire, and hopes breed feares,
    O onely obiect, for an Eagles eie,
    Whose light, and heate, make men to liue and die.

Twixt these, a daintie paradise doth lie,
As sweete as in the Sunne the Phenix Bowre,
As white as snowe, as smooth as Iuorie,
As faire, as Psyches bosome, in that howre,
    When she disclosde the boxe of Beauties Queene,
    All this and more, is in Sibilla seene.

T. W. Gent.

S Ir painter, are thy colours redie set,
    My Mistresse can not be with thee to day,
    Shee's gone into the field to gather May,
The timely Prymrose, and the Violet:
    Yet that thou maist, not disapointed bee,
    Come draw hir picture by my fantasee.

And well for thee, to paint hir by thine eare,
    For should thine eie, vnto that office serue,
    Thine Eie, and Hand, thy Art, & Hart, would swerue,
Such maiestie hir countenance doth beare,
    And where thou wert Apelles thought before,
    For failing so, thou shouldst be praisd no more.

Drawe first hir Front, a perfect Iuorie white,
    Hie, spatious, round, and smooth on either side,
    Hir temples brancht with vains, blew, opening wide.
As in the Map, Danubius runs in sight:
    Colour hir semicircled browes with iet,
    The throne where Loue triumphantly doth set.

Regard hir Eie, hir eie, a woondrous part,
    It woundeth deepe, and cureth by and by,
    It driues away, and draweth curteously,
It breeds and calmes, the tempest of the hart,
    And what to lightning Ioue, belongeth too,
    The same hir lookes, with more effect can doe.

Hir Cheeke, resembleth euerie kinde of way,
    The Lillie stainde, with sweete Adonis blood,
    As wounded he strai'd vp and downe the wood,
For whome faire Venus languisht many a day,
    Or plainly more to answere your demaune,
    Hir cheekes are Roses, ouercast with lawne.

Hir louely Lip, doth others all excell,
On whom it please (ay me) a kisse bestoe,
He neuer tasteth afterward of woe,
Such speciall vertue in the toutch doth dwell:
    The colour tempred of the morning red,
    Wherewith Aurora doth adorne hir head.

Hir ample Chest, an heauenly plot of ground,
The space betweene, a Paradise at least,
Parnassus like, hir twifolde mounting breast,
Hir heauenly graces, heapingly abound,
    Loue spreads his conquering colours in this feeld,
    Whereto the race of Gods and men doe yeeld.

The other parts, which custom doth conceale,
Within a sarcenet vaile thou must conuay,
So due proportion well discerne I may,
What though the garment doe not all reueale,

The shadow of a naked thigh may fraight,
His head brim full, hath any fine conceit.

Before hir Feete, vpon a Marble stone,
Inflamed with the Sunbeames of hir eie,
Depaint my hart that burneth passionately,
And if thy pensill can set downe such mone,
    Thy picture selfe, will teeling semblance make,
    Of ruthe and pitie for my torments sake.

How now Apelles, are thy senses tane?
Hast drawne a picture, or drawne out thy hart?
Wilt thou be held a Master of thine art,
And temper colours tending to thy bane?
    Happie my hart, that in hir Sunshine fries,
    Aboue thy hap that in hir shadow dies.

I Pray thee Loue, say, whither is this posting,
Since with thy deitie first I was acquainted,
I neuer saw thee thus distracted coasting,
    With countenance tainted.

Thy conquering arrowes broken in thy quiuer,
Thy brands that woont the inward marrow sunder,
Fireles and forceles, all a peeces shiuer,
    With mickle wonder.

That maketh next my staylesse thoughts to houer,
I cannot sound this vncouth cause of beeing,
The vaile is torne that did thy visage couer,
    And thou art seeing.

A stranger, one (quoth Loue) of good demerit,
Did sute and seruice to his Soueraine proffer,
In any case she would not seeme to heare it,
    But scornd the offer.

And very now vpon this Maying morrow,
By breake of day, he found me at my harbour,
I went with him, to vnderstand his sorrow,
                    Vnto hir Arbour.

Where he Loue torments dolefully vnfolded,
With words, that might a Tigers hart haue charmed,
His sighes and teares, the mountaine yee had moulted,
                      And she not warmed.

Hir great disdaine against hir Louer proued,
Kindled my brand, that to hir brest I seated,
The flame betweene hir paps, them often moued.
                      Nor burnt, nor heated.

My arrowes keene I afterward assaied,
Which from hir brest without effect rebounded.
And as a ball, on Marble floore they plaied,
                      With force confounded.

The brand that burnt, old Pryams Towne to asshes,
Now first his operation, wants it than,
The darts that Emerald skies in peeces dasshes,
                      Skornd by a woman.

Thus while I saide, she toward me arriued,
And with a tutch of triumph, neuer doubted,
To teare the vaile, that vse of sight bereaued,
                      So Loue was louted.

The vaile of error, from mine eies bereaued,
I sawe heauens hope, and earth hir treasurie,
Well maist thou erre said I, I am deceiued,
                      Bent to pleasure thee.

Cease haples man, my succors to importune,
Shee onely shee, my stratagemes repelleth,
Vainly endeuor I, to tempt hir Fortune,
                      That so excelleth.

Content thee, man, that thou didst see and suffer,
And be content, to suffer, see, and die,
And die content, bicause thou once didst mooue hir,
                        She displeasd thereby.

And herewithall I left the man a dyeng,
For by his passions I perceiu'd none other,
I hie me thus asham'd with speedie flyeng,
                        To tell my Mother.

FINIS

Authorship

Except where specified below, the authors are anonymous or unknown.

Poem N°	Author / Title *or* First Line	Page N°
3	Matthew Roydon, (fl. 1580–1622) / 'An Elegie, or friends passion, for his Astrophill.'	13
4	Sir Walter Raleigh, (?1552–1618) / 'An Epitaph vpon the right Honorable sir Philip Sidney knight: Lord gouernor of Flushing.'	20
5	*possibly* Fulke Greville, Lord Brooke, (1554–1628) / 'Another of the same.'	22
6	G.P. *Master of Arts* [*probably* George Peele, ?1558–?1597] / 'The praise of Chastitie.'	23
8–11	*N. B. Gent.* [Nicholas Breton, ?1545–?1626] /	
	'The Preamble to N.B. his Garden plot'	31
	'A strange description of a rare Garden plot.'	32
	'An excellent Dreame of Ladies and their Riddles.'	33
	'The Chesse Play.'	38
12	*probably* Robert Greene (?1558–1592) / 'A most rare, and excellent Dreame'	40
14–29	*T. L. Gent.* [Thomas Lodge, ?1558–1625] /	
	'Muses helpe me, sorrow swarmeth'	55
	'Striue no more'	58
	'Of ceasles thoughts my mind hath fram'd his wings'	58
	'When Pirrha made hir miracle of stones'	59
	'All day I weepe my wearie woes'	59
	'My fraile and earthly barke by reasons guide'	60
	'Midst lasting griefes, to haue but short repose'	61
	'Oh woods vnto your walks my bodie hies'	61
	'Accurst be loue and they that trust his traines'	63
	'Now I finde, thy lookes were fained'	63
	'The fatall starre that at my birthday shined'	64
	'Faine to content, I bend my selfe to write'	65
	'Full fraught with vnrecomptles sweete'	67
	'Like desart woods, with darksome shades obscured'	68
	'For pittie pretie eies surcease'	68
	'My bonie Lasse thine eie'	69
30	Sir Edward Dyer, (d. 1607) /	

	'Alas my hart, mine eie hath wronged thee'	70
31	*E. O.* [Edward de Vere, Earl of Oxford, 1550–1604] /	
	'What cunning can expresse'	71
32	*N. B. Gent.* [Nicholas Breton, ?1545–?1626] /	
	'A most excellent passion'	72
33	*Sir W. H.* [*poss.* Sir William Harbert, d. 1593] /	
	'These lines I send by waues of woe'	74
38	*possibly* Sir Walter Raleigh /	
	'Praisd be Dianas faire and harmles light'	77
39–40	Sir Walter Raleigh /	
	'Like to a hastrophillermite poore in place obscure'	78
	'Like truthles dreames, so are my ioyes expired'	79
44	Sir Walter Raleigh /	
	'Calling to minde mine eie long went about'	81
46	*Unknown,* [translation of Ronsard] /	
	'Would I were chaung'd into that golden showre'	82
48	*possibly* Nicholas Breton /	
	'Those eies that holds the hand of euery hart'	83
50	*possibly* Sir Edward Dyer, d. 1607 /	
	'As rare to heare, as seldome to be seene'	84
54	*W. S. Gent.* [*poss.* William Smith, fl. 1596] /	
	'A notable description of the World.'	86
59	*Unknown* [after Petrarch, *Rime* 145] /	
	'Set me where Phoebus heate, the flowers slaieth'	90
70	*possibly* Sir Edward Dyer /	
	'Diuide my times, and rate my wretched howres'	96
71	*possibly* Sir Walter Raleigh /	
	'A description of Loue.'	98
73	*possibly* Nicholas Breton /	
	'Ah poore Conceit, delite is dead'	100
75	*Unknown* [after Ariosto, *Orlando Furioso* I.42–43] /	
	'The praise of Virginitie.'	102
78–80	*T. W. Gent.* [Thomas Watson, ?1557–1592] /	
	'Aurora now, began to rise againe'	104
	'Away dispaire, the death of hopeles harts'	106
	'I hope and feare, that for my weale or woe'	107

Notes on the text

The original edition of *The Phoenix Nest* has some period aspects that have not been retained here, although every effort has been made to stay as close to that edition as possible, within the confines of modern typography. The changes are as follows:

- the long S—which looks like an 'f' with the right half of the horizontal stroke missing—has been represented by 's';
- where VV is used for W, the modern W has been preferred;
- the 'ct' ligature has been abandoned;
- where a vowel bears a tilde (an abbreviation indicating that the vowel should be read as being followed by 'n' or 'm', eg: frõ), the 'n' or 'm' has been silently added in accordance with modern custom, and the tilde removed.

With the above exceptions, all period spelling conventions have been respected. Where a letter or punctuation mark appears within square brackets, this indicates that it has been inserted by the modern editor to achieve the correct reading. Where spelling errors occur in the original, other than those involving missed letters, a marginal comment has been made as to the assumed correct reading. In the case of the drop caps that begin each poem, the style of the original has been followed exactly; thus, some poems begin with a three-line drop cap, although most begin with a two-liner. Where a larger one has been applied—five lines or more—this is a replacement for a decorated letter, in the style of an illuminated manuscript, which I have not sought to reproduce.

The main source for this edition is the Harvard University Press edition edited by Hyder E. Rollins (1931, reissued 1969). This has been compared with the PDF version made available online by Renascence Editions at: https://scholarsbank.uoregon.edu/xmlui/handle/1794/70 which in turn was transcribed by Greg Foster from the UMI microfilm copy of the edition held by the British Library at press-mark Huth 42, and with the the Scolar Press facsimile (ed. D. E. L. Crane, 1973) of the copy held in the Bodleian Library (shelfmark: Mal 287). In cases of doubt, Rollins' readings have been preferred.

Afterword

The Phœnix Nest was published in 1593, and went though only two editions—the second 21 years after the first—despite its importance, and despite the quality of the work that it offers.

No satisfactory identification of the compiler, R.S., has been made, and it must be assumed that he will remain no more than a pair of initials to literary history. It may safely be assumed that the phoenix of the title was the much-admired and widely-lionised Sir Philip Sidney, who had died in military service in the Netherlands, and to whom the opening elegies in the book are addressed. A popular figure at court, a daring adventurer, and a major poet, Sidney was every inch the Renaissance courtier. His verse was at the very forefront of the latest trends, above all in the adoption of the Pastoral mode, exemplified by his prose-and-verse masterpiece, *Arcadia*. Thomas Lodge (here *T. L. Gent.*) was evidently much influenced by Sidney's example. However, alongside such forward-looking figures, we also find Nicolas Breton (here, *N. B. Gent.*), an adherent of the earlier school of Surrey and Wyatt, both of whom had died during the reign of Henry VIII, some fifty years previously, and whose work had gained wider currency through *Tottel's Miscellany* (1557).

The Phoenix Nest is a rare volume, and given that it was only reprinted long after the first edition, one might assume that its impact at the time was limited, certainly by comparison with *England's Helicon* (1600), a compilation twice as long and entirely given over to Pastoral. It would nonetheless have been in the possession of a number of gentleman versifiers, given that its editor was himself a gentleman, and I suspect—with not a great deal of concrete evidence to sustain this—that the book may well have exerted considerable influence, thanks to the evident good taste of its compiler. It was a good book when published; it remains so to this day.

Tony Frazer
Exeter, 2009

Index of Titles and First Lines
(Titles in italics)

Accurst be loue and they that trust his traines	63
Ah poore Conceit, delite is dead	100
Alas my hart, mine eie hath wronged thee	70
All day I weepe my wearie woes	59
Another of the same	22
As ioy of ioyes, and neuer dying blis	90
As rare to heare, as seldome to be seene	84
As then, no winde at all there blew	13
Aurora now, began to rise againe	104
Away dispaire, the death of hopeles harts	106
Brainsicke race that wanton youth ensues, The	76
By wracke late driuen on shore, from Cupids Crare	86
Calling to minde mine eie long went about	81
Cease restles thoughts, surcharg'd with heauines	92
Chesse Play, The	38
Com yunglings com, that seem to make such mone	72
Counterloue, A	89
Dead mans Right, The	9
Declare O minde, from fond desires excluded	89
Description of Iealousie, The	99
Description of Loue, A	98
Diuide my times, and rate my wretched howres	96
Elegie, or friend's passion, for his Astrophill, An	13
Epitaph vpon the Right Honorable sir Philip Sidney, An	20
Excellent Dialogue betweene Constancie and Inconstancie, An	27
Excellent Ditties of diuers kindes	53
Excellent Dreame of Ladies and their Riddles, An	33
Faine to content, I bend my selfe to write	65
Fatall starre that at my birthday shined, The	64
Feede still thy selfe, thou fondling with beliefe	75
Firmament, with golden stars adorned, The	92
For pittie pretie eies surcease	68
Fvll fraught with vnrecomptles sweete	67
Gentle season of the yeere, The	87
Hir face, Hir tong, Hir wit	80
I hope and feare, that for my weale or woe	107

I Pray thee Loue, say, whither is this posting	109
I sawe the eies, that haue my seeing bounde	91
In Orchard grounds, where store of fruit trees grew	33
Like desart woods, with darksome shades obscured	68
Like to a Hermite poore in place obscure	78
Like truthles dreames, so are my ioyes expired	79
Midst lasting griefes, to haue but short repose	61
Most excellent passion set downe by N. B., Gent., A	72
Most rare, and excellent Dreame, A	40
Mvses help me, sorrow swarmeth	55
My bonie Lasse thine eie	69
My first born loue vnhappily conceiued	76
My fraile and earthly barke by reason's guide	60
My garden ground of griefe: where selfe wils seeds are sowne	32
Narcissus neuer by desire distressed	91
Noble Romans whilom woonted were, The	23
Notable description of the World, A	86
Now I find, thy lookes were fained	63
Now what is Loue, I praie thee tell	98
O Night, O ielious night, repugnant to my pleasures	102
O See my hart, vncertaine what effect	94
Oh woods vnto your walks my bodie hies	61
Of all the woes my pensiue hart endureth	96
Of ceasles thoughts my mind hath fram'd his wings	58
Of thick and thin, light, heauie, dark and cleere	86
Praise of Chastitie, The	23
Praise of Virginitie, The	102
Praisd be Dianas faire and harmles light	77
Preamble to N. B. his Garden plot, The	31
Preface to the Reader, A	8
Secret many yeeres vnseene, A	38
Secret murder hath bene done of late, A	79
Seeing friend yet enimie to rest, A	99
Seeing those eies, that with the Sun contendeth	95
Set me where Phoebus heate, the flowers slaieth	90
Short is my rest, whose toile is ouerlong	101
Silence augmenteth griefe, writing encreaseth rage	22
Sir painter are thy colours redie set	107
Sought by the world, and hath the world disdain'd	80

Strange description of a rare Garden plot, A	32
Strive no more, / forspoken ioyes to spring	58
Sweete fellow whom I sware, such sure affected loue	31
Sweete Violets (Loue's paradice) that spred	103
These lines I send by waues of woe	74
Thinking vpon the name by Loue engraued	93
Those eies that holds the hand of euery hart	83
Those eies which set my fancie on a fire	77
Though neither tears nor torments can be thought	85
Time, when first I fell in Loue, The	84
To make a truce, sweet Mistres with your eies	94
To praise thy life, or waile thy woorthie death	20
To shun the death, my rare and chosen Ieuell	95
Virginitie resembleth right the Rose	102
Weepe you my lines for sorrow whilst I write	53
What cunning can expresse / The fauor of hir face	71
What else is hell, but losse of blisfull heauen	81
When day is gone, and darknes come	85
When Pirrha made hir miracle of stones	59
While we sleepe, whereof may it proceed, The	40
Who list to heare the sum of sorrowes state	83
Who plucks thee down from hie desire poor hart?	82
Would I were chaung'd into that golden showre	82

www.ingramcontent.com/pod-product-compliance
Lightning Source LLC
Chambersburg PA
CBHW031156160426
43193CB00008B/389